LEAD SMART

5 KEYS OF LEADERSHIP SUCCESS

SANJAY BHATTACHARYA, PhD.

BLUEROSE PUBLISHERS
India | U.K.

Copyright © Sanjay Bhattacharya 2024

All rights reserved by author. No part of this publication may be reproduced, stored in a retrieval system or transmitted in any form or by any means, electronic, mechanical, photocopying, recording or otherwise, without the prior permission of the author. Although every precaution has been taken to verify the accuracy of the information contained herein, the publisher assume no responsibility for any errors or omissions. No liability is assumed for damages that may result from the use of information contained within.

BlueRose Publishers takes no responsibility for any damages, losses, or liabilities that may arise from the use or misuse of the information, products, or services provided in this publication.

For permissions requests or inquiries regarding this publication, please contact:

BLUEROSE PUBLISHERS
www.BlueRoseONE.com
info@bluerosepublishers.com
+91 8882 898 898
+4407342408967

ISBN: 978-93-5819-807-2

First Edition: January 2024

This book is dedicated to

My

Blessed Family

(The fountain of spur)

"So let's not get tired of doing what is good. At just the right time we will reap a harvest of blessing if we don't give up". - Galatians 6:9 (NLT)

Acknowledgement

It is really satisfying to bring out this book that contains strategic discussions on smart leadership, to be successful.

Any initiative is a set task and it would be imbalanced, if I do not recognize the support rendered by them. First of all, I lift up my heart to the God almighty whose guidance is constantly a light of lamp for my pathway.

In the process of writing this book, I have referred many literature, and cases of various eminent and distinguished writers. I have tried to acknowledge their contribution wherever possible. Notwithstanding the above, I do express my deep appreciation to my well-wishers who have encouraged me in this scholarly pursuit. In particular, I am obliged to all who have confirmed my work as an expression of their whole hearten concern and as such I express my recognition to them. Their words of endorsement are an encouragement and are published in this book. I would like to sincerely appreciate my friend Alfred Sudhakar Ling for helping me with the cover design of this book.

I owe a bottomless sense of gratitude to my blessed family members for the constant support and inspiration, which has been a source of insight to complete this book with full desire. As an appreciation, this book is dedicated to my family and their backup was of great value to me.

I am grateful to BlueRose Publishers for having uncovered interest in bringing out this book and do wish that this book complement the readers with a wide stretching understanding and information about the space under discussion.

Sanjay Bhattacharya

About the Book......

We desire to be successful in our capabilities to lead. In order to be successful we have to be smart enough to join hands with people, empathize with them, and connect with their aspirations in - managing people or heading a project; and inspire others to accomplish something important. Leaders set the patterns of behaviour and influences people in formation of constructive culture in the organization.

Leadership refers to somebody who can encourage, stimulate, and care others regardless of their position and power. We need smart leaders that take a stand and make difference in the lives of the people. People always looked for persons whom they can follow, learn from them, be inspired by them, and model them. We are all inclined to seek leadership at all levels. At times we work intensively with individual skills, aspirations, and behaviours; sometimes our focus is on design and delivery of results; at other times we support teams, whole organization or systems.

This book LEAD SMART outlines the key areas to leadership success. The topics included in this book help to self-reflect on these key areas of leadership success. The keys of leadership success are five Cs. They are - calling, competency, commitment, confidence, and compassion. There are seven chapters in this book LEAD SMART and are outlined as under:

Chapter 1: Smart leading is about staying grounded in certainty and lead from a position of strength. This chapter deliberates upon the five key essentials (Cs) of smart leadership that are – calling, competency, commitment, confidence, and compassion.

Chapter 2: A calling is a vocation or way of life that form a higher urge of inner feeling within self to be smart. This chapter discusses on the first C, i.e. "calling" and its four elements- purpose, talent, passion, and value.

Chapter 3: Competency is a cluster of knowledge, skills, and attitude underlying personal characteristics that drive resultant behaviour leading to success or superior performance on the job. This chapter discusses the second C, i.e. "competency" and its five elements- self-management, adaptability, strategic thinking, collaborative relationships, and achieving results. Once we understand our calling, we need to work on building our competency to be smart in excelling the performance for delivering the results.

Chapter 4: Leaders need to continually evaluate commitment to - their purpose, people they lead, and organization they work. A person may have the call and even competency to lead but if there is a lack in the commitment to drive the call and competency, s/he cannot be a smart leader. This chapter discusses the third C, i.e. "commitment" and its three elements- demonstration of continuous persistence by self, shape influence on others, and craving to the accomplishment of goals.

Chapter 5: Confident leaders are able to deal immediately in a smart manner with problems and conflicts directly; rather than pro-casting, ignoring, or passing problems to others. In spite of having a calling, developing our competencies, and having commitment towards accomplishment; it is necessary that the smart leader must be having the confidence to take responsible risks and accomplish higher goals. This chapter discusses about the fourth C, i.e. "confidence" and its three elements - positive thinking which includes, care for people and optimistic approach; have belief in self which includes, trust and sense of control; and take right decisions which includes, original view point and validated information; in leadership role.

Chapter 6: Compassionate leader, can encourage healthy relationships to ensure a more empathetic work environment. Once the leader works on the calling to build competency having commitment and developed confidence, it is necessary to have the compassionate heart to be a smart leader. This chapter discusses about the fifth C, i.e. "compassion". Some of the observed behaviour of compassionate leadership are – go from self to others, create a win-win situation, aspire to understand, learn from others, and exemplify positivity. These behaviours lead to mindfulness, listening ability, inspiring others, and inclusiveness; for achieving the desired results which are the four element of compassionate leadership.

Chapter 7: The framework of leadership presents set of rules, ideas, or beliefs which we use in order to deal with problems or to decide what to do within that context. The framework of our leadership has to be strategic in nature because it provides a self-improving blueprint that presents the interplay and consistency between an organization business strategy and various stakeholders. This chapter ponders upon the strategic framework of five key areas of smart leadership that includes- the objectives, indicators, assumptions, and expected outcomes of each key area to lead smart.

The central focus of this book is to lead smart and explore our capabilities on its five key areas. The perspectives discussed under these five key areas of smart leadership allows us to see our own potential as well as see the potential in the people we lead.

I have tried to present the ideas in simple language with unique relevant features like – discussion questions, relevant exercises, reflections, case analysis (though imaginary but related to real situations), self-assessment tools, action plan, leadership take away, and graphic of each relevant topic where ever required. All the 5 keys of leadership success discussed in this book are highly practical in nature to nurture us to lead smart. The practical focus of this book distinguishes it in the presentation style from currently available titles.

The target readers for this book are the people who are leading in corporate companies, not for profit organizations, development organizations, churches, mission organizations, etc. I have pointed out the integration of theory and practice in five areas of smart leadership for better understanding of the upcoming realities in regard to our leadership success.

I would welcome those who come out with practical suggestions and shall be duly acknowledged.

Happy Reading!!!

Sanjay Bhattacharya

Endorsements....

Followers of Jesus desiring to grow in their understanding and practice of Christian leadership would do well to read this book. Sanjay Bhattacharya guides readers on an exploration of five keys to fruitful service – calling, competency, commitment, confidence, and compassion – and does it in a clear, concise, and interactive manner. Check it out. See for yourself. You find thoughtful content coupled with case studies aimed at enhancing and enlivening your leadership. I particularly appreciated how the book concludes by challenging God's servants to assess their leadership in these five areas. In so doing, it helps readers put to use what they have learned and grow others in the process.

-Dr Gary G Hoag, President& CEO, Global Trust Partners, Denver, USA.

This book, -Lead Smart: 5 Keys to Leadership Success; written by Dr Sanjay Bhattacharya, is an excellent read for aspiring leaders. Dr Bhattacharya identifies calling, competency, commitment, confidence, and compassion as the primary traits of smart leadership based on his interactions with leaders and their teams in organisations ranging in size from very small to very large. Readers will be able to use these 5 Cs of smart leadership to evaluate their own management skills and identify areas for improvement.

-Rev. Viji Varghese Eapen, PhD (Dublin University, Ireland); Vicar, Church of South India.

It is a pleasure to know about Dr Sanjay Bhattacharya's upcoming publication "Lead Smart- 5 Keys of Leadership Success". I congratulate Dr Bhattacharya for painstakingly bringing up this very important subject to apply to our constantly changing society. We need confident, effective, and authentic leadership to lead our organizations to create solutions to complex problems. Having in-built competencies, a leader begins their journey with a calling who would have competency, commitment, and confidence with a compassionate outlook. The present book deals with these five smart qualities and sends a compelling message to aspiring leaders and influencers.

-Dr Santha Kumari Jetty, PhD, Ed.D; Public Policy Advocate, Educator, and Social Scientist; Columbus State University, Georgia, USA.

The world is in a state of greater flux than ever before. Technology has disrupted conventional ways of achieving results. The need for "Leading Smart" is greater today than ever before. Dr Sanjay Bhattacharya's book comes along at the right time to help leaders in leading in the current context. The five keys that the book digs into are bang on, and will transform anyone's leadership perspective and behaviour. The self-assessment tools, and the action plans that are included with every "C" will help the readers to know where they stand and help them to develop from there. Sanjay's thoroughness and academic rigour adds to the credibility of the concepts and the tool kits that he has gifted to the readers. I highly recommend Lead Smart to leaders at all levels.

-Dr Madna Kumar, Leadership Coach, Author, Servant Leadership Evangelist, Leadyne Organisation Builders, Bangalore, India.

I am delighted to know that Dr Sanjay Bhattacharya is publishing his book on the title- Lead Smart: 5 Keys of Leadership Success. Though books on leadership abound, a fresh look at leadership from different perspectives do matter. I liked the definition for Leading Smart – Being grounded and leading from the position of strength. The five Cs of leadership - calling, competency, commitment, confidence, and compassion, covered by the book also invited me to look forward to the book. I am sure that the book will revive existing leaders to be grounded and develop and nurture new leaders with the 5 Cs deeply ingrained in them.

-Dr Mercia Selva Malar, Associate Professor at Xavier Institute of Management and Entrepreneurship, Bangalore, India.

Contents

Chapter 1: Smart Leading 1

Chapter 2: Leading by Calling 25

Chapter 3: Leading by Competency 39

Chapter 4: Leading by Commitment 54

Chapter 5: Leading by Confidence 69

Chapter 6: Leading by Compassion 82

Chapter 7: Strategic Framework of Smart Leadership 100

Index 126

"One of the most important things about leadership is that you have to have the kind of humility that will allow you to be coached." -Jim Yong Kim

Chapter 1

Smart Leading

Introduction

Success is an ongoing realization and obtaining worthy desired results. Leadership is a very broad subject to talk about. Successful leaders are able to influence, by supporting their team or group of people they lead. It is important to point out that there is much more to leading successfully than just delegating from the top. Few examples of successful influential leaders are -Mahatma Gandhi, Oprah Winfrey, and Martin Luther King Jr. Understanding about exceptional leadership is beneficial because it allows us to learn positive traits and behaviours to emulate.

> *"A leader is one who knows the way, goes the way, and shows the way."* - **John C. Maxwell**

Discussion questions:

1. How would you describe your leadership style?
   _____
   _____
   _____

2. Think of a leader whom you have come across who take lead on accomplishing the task, but also like to stay involved and inspire the team by showing that s/he is working hands-on to help them, too.
   _____
   _____
   _____

A smart leader is someone who is not only in charge of organizing, guiding, and managing others but also join hand with the people and connects a team together through a common purpose. Leaders are expected to establish a vision, provide a plan of action, and build strong relationships with their followers. As a result, they empathize and guide people to accomplish incredible feats together. Their leading sets an example for people to accomplish positive changes because they lead as

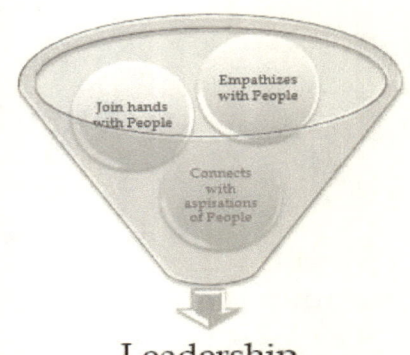

Leadership

visionary who motivate and encourage their team to reach the desired aspirations by contributing their best effort. Enabling strong relationships in the workplace allows for effective communication, more creativity, and better problem-solving skills.

"Leadership is all about the ability to join hands with people, empathize with them, and connect with their aspirations in leading."
- Sanjay Bhattacharya, PhD

Therefore, leading successfully is not just about delegation. It is necessary to work alongside with the people we lead by joining hands with them, understand them well to empathize, and creating opportunities connecting with their aspirations. Successful leaders combine these things together in influencing others towards the accomplishment of common goals.

Key Essentials of Smart Leading

A team looks towards the leader to lead them successfully and the leader does not assume a leadership role simply because someone hands them a title; instead a smart leader is an influencer who can work along with the people, understand their mind, and lead them to achieve their aspirations for putting their efforts to get the best out of their people for the common goals.

"If your actions inspire others to dream more, learn more, do more and become more, you are a leader." - **John Quincy Adams**

A leader, to be successful has to be smart in learning from the life situations to get things right by choosing the right approach at the right time. They averse to failure and show lot of intelligence with the ability to learn, understand things, deal with the situations, and rise to the occasion; with the right response, the right decision, and the right direction.

Smart leading is about staying grounded in certainty and lead from a position of strength. Potential advantages of being smart rather than right, includes- being able to achieve our goals, being more persuasive, having better interpersonal relationships, and learning to think through situations rather than act on impulse. They grow capacity to meet the demands of the moment and the challenges of the future.

The five keys of smart leading are discussed as under:

1. **Calling:** The first key essential for leading smart is "calling". A calling is a vocation or way of life that form a higher urge of inner feeling within self. When we know our calling we 'find our vocation' and 'follow our dreams'. This is a phrase we can hear in both social and professional contexts. Our calling drives us to grow into our own authentic self-hood irrespective of the fact what others think about us to be. People who feel a connection between their personal values and passion generally see their job as a calling. They firm up their commitment to succeed in leveraging their talents for achieving the superior purpose. This is because they want to see the bigger picture of what they are doing. Therefore, calling helps to discover and align our values, passion, talents, and purpose of life.

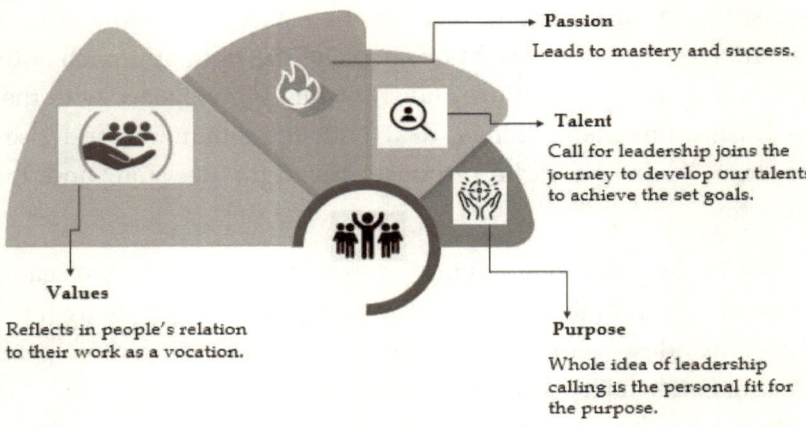

> *"The growth and development of people is the highest calling of leadership."* **- Harvey S. Firestone**

In leadership role we may choose to be a- pastor, professor, lawyer, engineer, doctor, para medical person, corporate person; or even as an individual member in a group/family, but the effectiveness of the person depends upon the calling which is the first key to be a smart leader.

2. **Competency:** The second key essential to be a smart leader is "competency". Once we understand our calling, we need to work on building our competency to excel in performance for delivering the results. Competency is a cluster of knowledge, skills, and attitude underlying personal characteristics that drive resultant behavior leading to success or superior performance on the job.

> *"Leadership is practiced not so much in words as in attitude and in actions."* **- Harold S. Geneen**

Leaders play an important role in demonstrating conduct, compliance, considerations, shared responsibilities, and outcomes. They have to ensure not only better job performance but also influence general understanding and satisfaction of all in the organization. They are the role models for others, hence they are supposed to manage themselves by adjusting to the changing environment, think strategically in taking right decisions, and sustain relationship with all stakeholders to achieve individual, team, or organizational goals & objectives. Therefore, leadership competency is a band of knowledge, skills, and attitude required to influence others with self-management, adaptability, strategic thinking, collaborative relationships, and achieving results. Competency is the second key after calling; to be a smart leader.

3. **Commitment:** The third key essential to become a smart leader is "commitment". A person may have the call and even competency to lead but if there is a lack in the commitment to drive the call and competency, s/he cannot be a smart leader. Leadership commitment is about -demonstration of continuous persistence by self, shape influence on others, and craving to the accomplishment of goals.

   A committed leader continues to move forward, looking for solutions, and working toward success. This persistent quality confronts challenges and retain our perspective even when the challenges of leadership become stressful or complicated. It can take years to become successful, with persistence playing a vital role in the process.

   > *"It is better to lead from behind and to put others in front, especially when you celebrate victory when nice things occur. You take the front line when there is danger. Then people will appreciate your leadership."*- **Nelson Mandela**

   An effective leader moves followers into action not with coercion but by eliciting their desire and conviction in the vision & goals through articulation.

   When we commit to the people and things that are truly important to us, our career, or our organization; the results are that our relationships with people will improve, we will be more 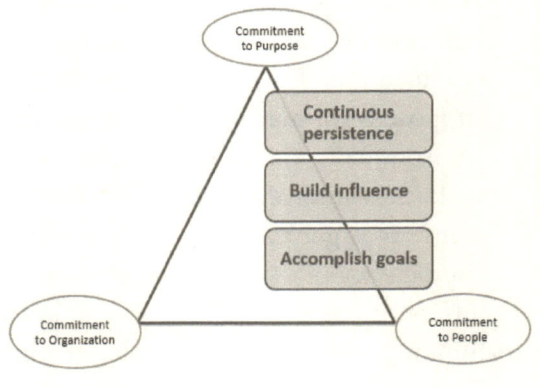 successful in achieving our goals, and we will have more time to enjoy our journey. Leadership commitment plays an important role for the achievement of the goals. Commitment urges us gradually to explore ourselves because it is a source to transform a capacity into a reality. The belief in our inner self is the foundation of commitment that makes us closer to the accomplishment of goals.

Commitment is an intelligent emotional bond of accomplishment. Leaders need to continually evaluate commitment to - their purpose, people they lead, and organization they work.

Therefore, leadership commitment is for the purpose, people, and organization. The commitment is developed though continuous persistence, to build influence, and accomplish goals. Commitment is the third key after calling and competency; to be a smart leader.

4. **Confidence:** The fourth key essential to grow as a smart leader is "confidence". In spite of having a calling, developing our competencies, and having commitment towards accomplishment; it is necessary that the leader must be having the confidence to take responsible risks and accomplish higher goals. Confident leaders are able to deal immediately in a smart manner with problems and conflicts directly; rather than pro-casting, ignoring, or passing problems to others. Confidence in leadership is to remain true to themselves and their values with integrity as they take responsibility for moving ahead to achieve results. They are visionaries, motivators, and encouragers.

"Most businesses think that product is the most important thing, but without great leadership, mission and a team that deliver results at a high level, even the best product won't make a company successful."
- *Robert Kiyosaki*

Confident leaders envision positive outcomes no matter what the situation may be. They believe that they have the talent and abilities to lead through an issue for positively impacting the people, team, or organization. They generally tend to have a positive outlook on life, and they have a strong belief in themselves. This belief allows them to take responsible risks and persevere through failures while all the while believing that goals will happen eventually. They constantly shape and guide individuals while making right decisions to keep moving. Therefore, confident leaders process positive thinking which includes- care for people and optimistic approach; have belief in self which includes -trust and sense of control; and take right decisions which includes -original view point and validated information; in leadership role. Confidence is the fourth key after calling, competency and commitment; to be a smart leader.

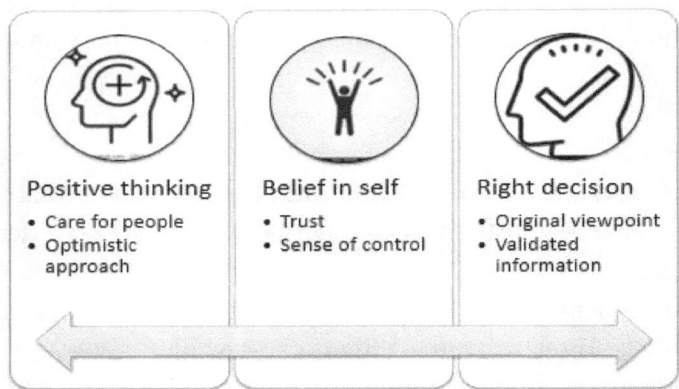

5. **Compassion:** The fifth key essential to lead smartly is "compassion". This is because even if they are stuck in some bad situation, they should be able to respond to the situation positively and show compassion to people.

Once the leader works on the calling to build competency having commitment and developed confidence; it is necessary to have the compassionate heart to be a smart leader. Compassionate leader, can encourage healthy relationships to ensure a more empathetic work environment.

"Leadership is unlocking people's potential to become better." **- Bill Bradley**

Compassionate leaders always put other's needs before their own. They recognize that every team member is unique and also an essential thread in the fabric of an entire team or organization. They strive to enhance the happiness and well-being of their people by supporting them with what they need to excel.

Compassionate leadership is focused on what is best for the individual, the team, and the organization in the long-term. Today, leaders are expected to treat their people with a greater sense of care and humanity to respect the unique attributes and qualities each person bring to the table. It means identifying ourselves with others and being mindful by seeing them as a part of team or organization and relating to what they are experiencing at a much deeper level. Compassionate leader expresses recognition by listening to people. Subsequently they are gratified and cared through support, mentorship, and guidance. People feel inspired to accomplish great things for themselves, their team, or the organization. Compassionate leadership foster people to work together with inclusiveness because of what their leadership mean for the people.

Therefore, some of the observed behavior of compassionate leadership are – go from self to others, create a win-win situation, aspire to understand, learn from others, and exemplify positivity. These behaviors lead to mindfulness, listening ability, inspiring others, and inclusiveness; for achieving the desired results. Compassion is the fifth key after calling, competency, commitment, and confidence; to be a smart leader.

Conclusion

Smart leaders possess vocation, capability, pledge, self-reliance, and empathy. These factors make them to be   self-aware of themselves and garner credibility. They sharpen their skills and are devoted to the task. They exhibit coolness focusing on relationship-building with humility.

Therefore, the key essentials of a smart leader are 5Cs - calling, competency, commitment, confidence, and compassion. Smart leaders are the role models to lead people, team, or organization.

"Leadership is not about titles, positions or flowcharts. It is about one life influencing another." -John C Maxwell

The 5 Cs of leading smart works in progressive order comprising of - calling; calling contributing to competency; competency contributing to commitment; commitment contributing to confidence; and, confidence contributing to compassion. These key dynamics altogether brands us as smart leaders adding value to empower others, stay authentic, and present ourselves as constant and consistent.

Reflection:

- Assess and deliberate on the way to improve on the elements of leading smart, using the given tools.
- Please indicate your answers by rating the indicators in the scale of 1-4 that best describes your view. Would you say you are-
  1 – Rarely
  2 – Occasionally
  3 – Often
  4- Always
- The more truly and honestly you rate each indicator, the more useful this assessment will be to your leadership development.
- Once the assessment is done using the tools, state the action required for yourself to address the gaps (where the score is below 4) in each element of key areas.

Use these tools below for each key area:

Table 1. Self –Assessment of Calling

Key Area	Element	Indicator	Score (1-4)
Calling	Values	I am able to reflect my values in relation to my role as a vocation.	
	Passion	I understand that leadership is not a destination, it is a journey and therefore I continue to refine, develop, and build from the foundation.	
	Talent	I am able to develop my talents and exhibit the characteristics most valuable to achieve the set goals.	
	Purpose	I am able to align my role with the overall objectives of the organization or group.	
	Total Score		
	(To find average, divide total by 4 and round to nearest whole number) **Average**		

Table 2. Self –Assessment of Competency

Key Area	Element	Indicator	Score (1-4)
Competency	Self-management	I am aware of myself and able to demonstrate ethics and integrity while performing my role.	
	Adaptability	I clearly understand the organization mission, vision, values, and strategy; to communicate and implement.	
	Strategic thinking	I am able to balance tension that occurs between strategic actions and daily tasks that will have a long-term impact on the organization.	
	Collaborative relationships	I have strong interpersonal skills that promote communication and contributing to the overall morale of a team or group.	
	Achieving results	I am able to evaluate and determine high potential people in the team to deliver results by building their capacity to promote a feeling of fairness among them who may wish to be considered for advancement.	
	Total Score		
		(To find average, divide total by 5 and round to nearest whole number) **Average**	

Table 3. Self –Assessment of Commitment

Key Area	Element	Indicator	Score (1-4)
Commitment	Continuous persistence	I am able to be persistent towards my goal or vision that keeps me driving for a higher purpose.	
	Build influence	I am able to influence others by my hard work, out of loyalty.	
	Accomplish goals	I constantly make new goals or vision and attempt to push my boundaries to achieve more.	
	Total Score		
	(To find average, divide total by 3 and round to nearest whole number) **Average**		

Table 4. Self –Assessment of Confidence

Key Area	Element	Indicator	Score (1-4)
Confidence	Positive thinking	Positive action keeps me motivated in achieving my goals by managing challenges better and learning from mistakes.	
	Belief in self	I believe in myself about the ability of my team or group for the future course of action and take responsible risks to achieve my personal and professional goals.	
	Right decision	I enter into the right decision-making process with an open mind and do not let my own biases influence them.	
	Total Score		
	(To find average, divide total by 3 and round to nearest whole number) **Average**		

Table 5. Self –Assessment of Compassion

Key Area	Element	Indicator	Score (1-4)
Compassion	Mindfulness	I have tremendous willingness to communicate with others more mindfully giving room for them to express themselves.	
	Listening	I listen to others and make them feel important as an individual.	
	Inspiring	I gain trust and confidence of others to enthuse them by showing them the willingness to put forth the same effort being asked by others.	
	Inclusiveness	I guide people to perform at a high level of excellence by creating a culturally inclusive framework where people work effectively across all functions for collective good.	
	Total Score		
	(To find average, divide total by 6 and round to nearest whole number) **Average**		

- Write down the average score of all the key areas and make the broad action plan for the weakest area to show how you will address the areas in which capability need to be built.

Use the appropriate template below:

Action Plan for Calling

Key Area	Average score	Element(s)/ Critical indicator(s)	What	Why	How	When
Calling		**Values:** I am able to reflect my values in relation to my role as a vocation.				
		Passion: I understand that leadership is not a destination, it is a journey and therefore I continue to refine, develop, and build from the foundation.				
		Talent: I am able to develop my talents and exhibit the characteristics most valuable to achieve the set goals.				
		Purpose: I am able to align my role with the overall objectives of the organization or group.				

- Use this template for action plan, if the weakest area of smart leadership is- calling (if the average score is lowest for this area).
- Look into the self-assessment score of the respective indicators under the element of calling.
- While making the action plan deliberate upon -what action steps are required under each indicator of the respective element, why it is necessary, how you will do, and by when you would like to address the gaps identified?
- Follow through the action steps.

Action Plan for Competency

Key Area	Average score	Element(s)/ Critical indicator(s)	What	Why	How	When
	Action plan for improving the week area(s) of smart leadership					
Competency		**Self-awareness:** I am aware of myself and able to demonstrate ethics and integrity while performing my role.				
		Adaptability: I clearly understand the organization mission, vision, values, and strategy; to communicate and implement.				
		Strategic thinking: I am able to balance tension that occurs between strategic actions and daily tasks that will have a long-term impact on the organization.				
		Collaborative relationships: I have strong interpersonal skills that promote communication and contributing to the overall morale of a team or group.				
		Achieving results: I am able to evaluate and determine high potential people in the team to deliver results by building their capacity to promote a feeling of fairness among them who may wish to be considered for advancement.				

- Use this template for action plan, if the weakest area of smart leadership is- competency (If the average score is lowest for this area).
- Look into the self-assessment scored of the respective indicators under the element of competency.
- While making the action plan deliberate upon -what action steps are required under each indicator of the element, why it is necessary,

how you will do, and by when you would like to address the gaps identified?
- Follow through the action steps.

Action Plan for Commitment

Action plan for improving the week area(s) of smart leadership						
Key Area	Average score	Element(s)/Critical indicator(s)	What	Why	How	When
Commitment		**Continuous persistence:** I am able to be persistent towards my goal or vision that keeps me driving for a higher purpose.				
		Build influence: I am able to influence others by my hard work, out of loyalty.				
		Accomplish goals: I constantly make new goals or vision and attempt to push my boundaries to achieve more.				

- Use this template for action plan, if the weakest area of smart leadership is- commitment (If the average score is lowest for this area).
- Look into the self-assessment scored of the respective indicators under the element of commitment.
- While making the action plan deliberate upon -what action steps are required under each indicator of the element, why it is necessary, how you will do, and by when you would like to address the gaps identified?
- Follow through the action steps.

Action Plan for Confidence

Key Area	Average score	Element(s)/Critical indicator(s)	What	Why	How	When
	Action plan for improving the week area(s) of smart leadership					
Confidence		**Positive thinking:** Positive action keeps me motivated in achieving my goals by managing challenges better and learning from mistakes.				
		Belief in self: I believe in myself about the ability of my team or group for the future course of action and take responsible risks to achieve my personal and professional goals.				
		Right decision: I enter into the right decision-making process with an open mind and do not let my own biases influence them.				

- Use this template for action plan, if the weakest area of smart leadership is-confidence (If the average score is lowest for this area).
- Look into the self-assessment scored of the respective indicators under the element of confidence.
- While making the action plan deliberate upon -what action steps are required under each indicator of the element, why it is necessary, how you will do, and by when you would like to address the gaps identified?
- Follow through the action steps.

Action Plan for Compassion

Action plan for improving the week area(s) of smart leadership							
Key Area	Average score	Element(s)/Critical indicator(s)	What	Why	How	When
Compassion		**Mindfulness:** I have tremendous willingness to communicate with others more mindfully giving room for them to express themselves.				
		Listening: I listen to others and make them feel important as an individual.				
		Inspiring: I gain trust and confidence of others to enthuse them by showing them the willingness to put forth the same effort being asked by others.				
		Inclusiveness: I guide people to perform at a high level of excellence by creating a culturally inclusive framework where people work effectively across all functions for collective good.				

- Use this template for action plan, if the weakest area of smart leadership is- compassion (If the average score is lowest for this area).
- Look into the self-assessment scored of the respective indicators under the element of compassion.
- While making the action plan deliberate upon -what action steps are required under each indicator of the element, why it is necessary, how you will do, and by when you would like to address the gaps identified?
- Follow through the action steps.

LEADERSHIP TAKEAWAY

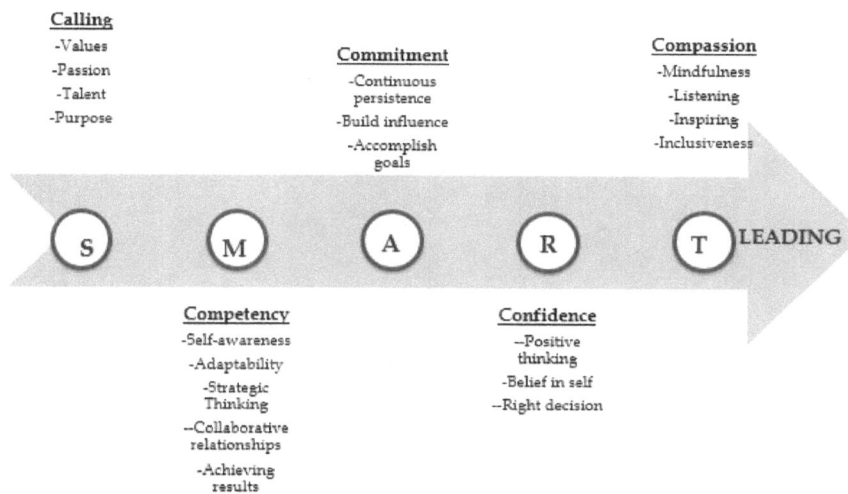

References:

1. **Jiyoung Park, Kyoungsu Lee, Jung in Lim, and Young Woo Sohn;** *Leading With Callings: Effects' of Leaders' Calling on Followers 'Team Commitment, Voice Behavior , and Job Performance; Front Psychol., 2018.*

2. **Sevy, Bruce:** *Identifying Competencies That Matter, leadership assessment products for PDI Ninth House.*

3. **Hopkin, Michael Ray**: *How to lead with commitment; https://leadonpurposeblog.com/2017/03/27/how-to-lead-with-commitment/, (March 27, 2017).*

4. **Bonds, Regina:** *Five signs you're leading with confidence, Chief Executive Insights, CEOWORLD Magazine; March 2022.*

5. **Worline, M and Dutton, JE:** *Awakening compassion at work: The quiet power that elevates people and organizations. Berrett-Koehler Publishers, (2017).*

"A successful life is one that is lived through understanding and pursuing one's own path, not chasing after the dreams of others."
- Chin-Ning Chu

Chapter 2

Leading by Calling

Introduction

Leadership should be a direct response to our calling. The calling of a true leader is to make a meaningful and lasting impact on the lives of people. Leadership can be looked differently based on our jobs or our role in other facets of the society. It can be seen by leading others in management positions of the organization or within our families, or social groups; we serve. We may have never been called a leader or we do not like leading others, but we still have the opportunity to influence and impact those we work with or will work with us in the future. Whatever our role may be, it is important to understand that we are having an impact on those around us. Leadership is the most powerful human force. The rewarding part of our calling as an educator, social worker, entrepreneur, lawyer, medical professional, or a coach; is that we too can see the impact we have on others while leading others as a fulfillment of our calling.

*"If your actions inspire others to dream more, learn more, do more, and become more, you are a leader." — **John Quincy Adams***

No job should be seen as too important or irrelevant because it all relates back to how we are doing our jobs and impacting others. And here is why we need to answer the call to lead smartly. A leader with a calling is likely to promote followers' behaviour based on a strong sense of connectedness, and followers' job performance is also likely to be influenced by leader's calling.

Discussion questions:

1. What is that you feel good about yourself? How is it aligned to your values to give you a self- identity as a person you are called to be?

_____

_____

_____

2. Which of your passions adds the most for the purpose of your life and leadership?

_____

_____

_____

3. What could you do to increase your talent to fulfil your calling?

_____

_____

_____

4. Who in your life seems to be the leader with a calling? What drives them to maintain what they do? (If you do not know, you can ask them.)

_____

_____

_____

Elements of Calling in Leadership

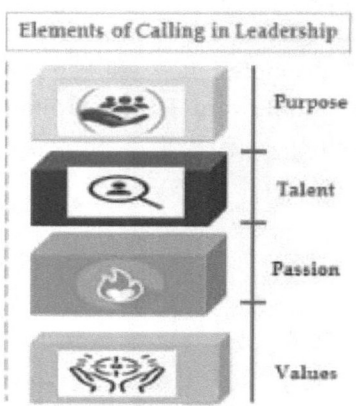

People who feel a connection between their personal values and passion generally see their job as a calling. They firm up their commitment to succeed in leveraging their talents for achieving the superior purpose. This is because they want to see the bigger picture of what they are doing.

The leaders with a calling exhibit a sense of ethics with aspirations to use their abilities for achieving the drive that satisfies every aspect of their lives.

"Calling in leadership is alignment of personal values with passion, committed to the success by leveraging the God given talent, contributing to superior purpose."- Sanjay Bhattacharya, PhD.

Hence calling entails the following elements in leadership:

1. **Values-** People want to work for a leader they can trust as a person of integrity with high moral values. Values are the core beliefs and principles that guide us in our calling to lead. It is reflected in personal as well as professional lives. Our values can be defined as the things we believe are most important to achieving our goals. Every organization or group has a set of core values, whether or not they are written down. The values guide the perspective of the organization or group as well as its actions.

    "Leadership is an opportunity to serve. It is not a trumpet call to self-importance."- J. Donald Walters

    The leaders who view their work as a calling also influence others at work. They are also accountable for follower commitment and behavior. Leadership values reflects in people's relation to their work as a vocation to goal accomplishment that enables meaningful insights and determination.

2. **Passion-** Passionate leaders are inclined to do something which is very important and close to their heart. They are called to be fully engaged and committed to achieving the shared goals. Leaders with a call continue to refine, develop, and build from their foundation because they understand leadership is not a destination, it is a journey. Passion elevates productivity and ensures followers are commitment to their vision.

"Outstanding leaders go out of their way to boost the self-esteem of their personnel. If people believe in themselves, it's amazing what they can accomplish." - **Sam Walton**

Eventually passion leads to mastery and success, because they are always thinking and working on the thing for which they are passionate about. Their calling is as much as their dream to achieve something they want or craving for.

3. **Talent-** Leadership calling is destined to their talents, and their talents are somehow considered interchangeably as their gifts. When we fail to nurture our God-given talents, we starve our seed of destiny. A calling is the inner urge to exploit our potentials. Our call for leadership joins the journey to develop our talents and exhibit the characteristics most valuable to achieve the set goals.

"I think one of the keys to leadership is recognizing that everybody has gifts and talents. A good leader will learn how to harness those gifts toward the same goal." **-Benjamin Carson**

People are the most valuable asset to help the organization or group reach where it needs to go in the future. The talents of leaders with a call need to be leveraged for inspiring others towards a vision, learning, and sustain leadership culture.

4. **Purpose-** Calling gives us the sense that we are evolving according to a larger life design – a realization that makes our lives feel purposeful. The purpose allows leaders to align their roles with the overall objectives of the organization or group. The purpose unites people in giving meaning to the goals we are striving to achieve together. The whole idea of leadership calling is the personal fit for the purpose.

"A good objective of leadership is to help those who are doing poorly to do well and to help those who are doing well to do even better." **- Jim Rohn**

A called leader refrain from activities that dilutes the purpose. The purpose fit can be ensured when leaders are able to lead by example, which is doing the right thing for the right reasons and without compromising with core values of the organization or group.

Conclusion

Leadership is hard to define as it means different things to different people. The core of leadership is to influence, help and guide others achieve goals that will ultimately fulfil a vision.

> *"At the heart of great leadership is a curious mind, heart, and spirit."*
> *- Chip Conley*

Leadership work is a dedication, a gift, and a mystery in the surrounding world of the marketplace. The tasks of smart leading call for the mind-set of the artist because leading is a learned art that comes through our values, passion, talent, and purpose. We must continually remind ourselves that our lives and our partners' and followers' lives are not problems to be solved. They are callings to be answered, and mysteries to be lived. Great leadership calling requires openness and responsiveness to the nitty-gritties of people we influence.

Reflection:

- Evaluate your leadership calling in each of the four elements (values, passion, talent, and purpose) mentioned and firm up your response to the stated questions:

Use the tool below-
  i. Who am I?
  ii. Who shall I be?
  iii. Is leading my calling?
  iv. When did I sense the call to lead?
  v. When did I fully commit to leading?

- **Leadership Calling exercise for element of Values:**

Values- Here is the list of few values. You may add more to the list. Quickly read through the list and place a tick (√) mark by any of the values that are important to you. Then go back and chose your five most important values and write them down and prioritize them in order as top values.

Accountability	Fun	Personal development
Adaptability	Generosity	Peace
Affection	Growth	Persistence
Authenticity	Harmony	Power
Belonging	Happiness	Prestige
Caring	Hard work	Productivity
Collaboration	Honesty	Quality
Commitment	Hospitality	Recognition
Compassion	Influence	Relationships
Control	Initiative	Resilience
Courtesy	Innovation	Respect
Creativity	Integrity	Responsibility
Dedication	Interdependence	Service
Discipline	Joy	Simplicity
Duty	Justice	Sincerity
Efficiency	Learning	Synergy
Empathy	Love	Teamwork
Equality	Loyalty	Trust
Excellence	Openness	Vision
Fairness	Order	Wisdom
Freedom	Originality	
Flexibility	Passion	
Friendship	Patience	

1.-------------,2.--------------,3.---------------,4.----------------,5.---------------------

These values should now inform your choices, decisions, you problem-solving opportunities, and more

- **Leadership Calling exercise for element of Passion:**

Passion- Identify three passions form the list below or any other passion you have that describes the way you interact with people. You may more to the list.

Being true to myself.	Leading from the front.
Empowering or helping others.	Motivating others towards goal.
Being confident in my own judgment & decisions.	Encouraging to perform.
Reading to gain new insights.	Inspiring other.
Teaching others for growth and development.	Learning something new.
Studying to understand.	Planning for achievement.
Managing things and people.	Selling ideas or product.

- **Leadership Calling exercise for element of Talent:**

Talent- Rank your three skills/abilities from the list below or any other skills which you feel good about you. You may add more to the list.

Deal with failure.	Emotional management
Be focused	Empathy building
Handle change	Problem solving
Make friends	Interpersonal relationship
Spot new trends	Stress management
Articulate	Art
Awareness	Finance
Communication	Strategic thinking
Computer literacy	Human Resource management
Conflict resolution	Inventiveness
Creativity	Leadership
Critical thinking	Marketing
Decision making	Story Telling
Writing	Singing
Networking	Visualization

- **Leadership Calling exercise for element of Purpose:**

Purpose-

Answer the following questions to determine your purpose	
What is my personal /professional identity?	
What are my most important objectives in life in my personal /professional identity?	
What specific activities/initiatives will lead me to achieve my objectives?	

After answering these questions in brief, develop a short statement of your purpose like examples below:

My purpose is to......

- To lead people to new realms of health, living or accomplishment.
- To create new ways of thinking.
- To nurture key relationships.
- To compassionately and intuitively work with people.
- To empower others to create and use their minds.
- To help others see the other side.
- To discover and apply new scientific truths, knowledge.
- To inspire others to offer their lives to the highest ideal.
- To build, organize and plan a large project.
- To resolve injustices.

- **Leadership Call Statement:**

Visualize your leadership calling by combining one or two of your values, passion, talent, and purpose; and define your perfect leadership calling.
My leadership calling is aligned   to_____(1 or 2 key values)   to_____(Passions   *that describes me)*   by   _____(applying/using   *1 or 2 talents)*   in order to _____   *(identified purpose).*

Case Analysis

Leadership Calling on People Management

Introduction

A new President was hired to lead a large, non-profit organization called, ABC, which provides education and advocacy to the citizens. Prior to this job at ABC, she worked for an international relief agency and travelled extensively in the field offices, managing its daily operations.

Her life experiences of growing up as a refugee, fuelled her motivation and passion for developmental work. It also shaped her values and working style. She is known to her colleagues as a person with clear purpose to lead the organization as "go-getter" and a "high performer."

The board of trustees thought her international experiences and talents like goal-oriented, and achievement-focused attitude was just what they needed; to expand the organization on a national level. The board wanted to hire a leader with a calling like her who can challenge people and push the organization to reach its goals.

Issue

Since her hire as President, employee productivity and motivation decreased due to a shift in the perceived leadership style by the people as compared to the erstwhile President. There was no enthusiasm among the people for the mission of the organization and the vision for the new work that she and the directors created in a strategic planning meeting. She had a staff meeting, and the majority of staff sauntered in late. Throughout the meeting, they gave her blank stares, and, as soon as the meeting was over, they quickly left. She was tired of the staff attitudes and behaviours, and determined to change it.

Action

As the newly appointed President, she took a look at her self-concept to know how it differs or corresponds with her people. The knowledge she gained about herself and others bridged her understanding of individual cultural differences, and how they are expressed in an organization. She built into her personal development plan to observe and listen to her people, thus helped her pay attention to her surroundings. By actively listening to her people, she learned how to adapt her behaviour appropriately for the situation she is in.

Being highly talented with the leadership call to be resilient, she developed her passion and purpose to make a difference in achieving the goal. It was probably because of her experience as a refugee. This also helped her to keep her values and stay positive about the situation.

Impact

She could improve on is her ability to measure the emotions of her people during their interactions. She used the power of words and language, share stories of herself, her vision, and where she would like the organization to be. She combined her stories with the stories of her people to create a unified story.

As a leader with a call, she recognized that cultural shifts can be difficult, and it is her responsibility as a leader to help her people, and make the changes successfully. She helped to adapt change cultural behaviour through the use of her stories.

Her leadership style was task- and goal-oriented, and is influenced by her upbringing. Later she was able to move the people commitment towards organization's accountability, goals, and achievement.

Discussion

1. What make the newly appointed President to be a leader with a call in influencing people commitment?
2. What values, passion, talents, and purpose are drawn in her leadership calling?

LEADERSHIP TAKEAWAY

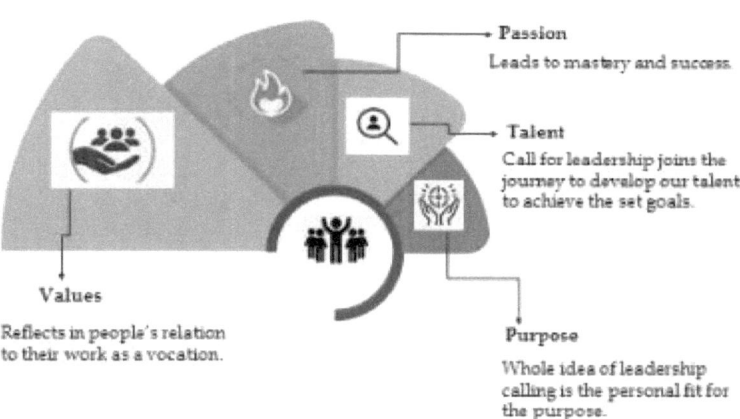

References:

1. **Tiago Esteves, Mitguel Pereira Lopes, Rosa Lutete Geremias, Patrica Jardim Palma;** Calling for leadership: leadership relation with worker's sense of calling; Leadership & Organization Development Journal, April 2018, (ISSN: 0143-7739).

2. **Jiyoung Park, Kyoungsu Lee, Jung in Lim, and Young Woo Sohn;** Leading With Callings: Effects' of Leaders' Calling on Followers 'Team Commitment, Voice Behavior, and Job Performance; Front Psychol., 2018.

"Success comes from knowing your purpose in life, growing to your maximum potential, & sowing seeds to benefit others."
-John C Maxwell

Chapter 3

Leading by Competency

Introduction

Competence is a standardized requirement for an individual to properly perform a specific job. More generally, competence is the state or quality of being adequate or well qualified; having the ability to perform a specific role. It encompasses a combination of knowledge, skills, and attitude utilized to improve performance. The ability to do something efficiently and effectively is the general characteristic of a successful competent person. This level of proficiency is not achieved overnight, but gradually through intentional success habits of sharpening the tools required to thrive. We need to get better at what we do; by building knowledge, skills, and attitude. And then to practice it over and over again till we reach our best.

> *"Give me six hours to chop down a tree and I will spend the first four sharpening the axe."* - **Abraham Lincoln.**

Competency is a cluster of knowledge, skills, and attitude, underlying personal characteristics that drive resultant behavior leading to success or superior performance on the job.

Components of Competency

Competency may be generic, or managerial, or functional/technical. Individuals need to have some information about the specific work area and also the ability to perform that work which may be mental or physical; and subsequently think about the actions, motives, and drives that direct to handpick the right behavior. Therefore, individuals should educate him/herself to build the knowledge, skills, and attitude; to work and outshine in performing that job.

> *"Education is the most powerful weapon which you can use to change the world." - **Nelson Mandela.***

Competency is the cumulative result of the interplay between three components. These components are:

- Knowledge- helps to build the skills.
- Skills - helps the knowledge to be exhibited.
- Attitude - helps in a pattern of actions based on the knowledge and skills of an individual.

The value of a leader is determined by the success of their entire team. Smart leaders have a critical role to play in providing strategic direction and creating an environment which enables people in the organization to develop for being more effective and agile. This work stream increases the capability and success of leaders, in order to drive organizational health, performance, and talent.

Discussion questions:

1. In what ways do you currently feel the strain of leadership within yourself?

   _____
   _____
   _____

2. What do you need to change to see yourself as someone with that competency?

   _____
   _____
   _____

3. What is one competency you have tried to develop in your leadership role?

   _____
   _____
   _____

4. Which of your current leadership competencies adds the most value to your life?

   _____
   _____
   _____

5. Whom do you consider to be a competent leader in your life? What drives them to be a competent leader?

   _____
   _____
   _____

Elements of Competency in Leadership

In order to lead other people smartly, we have to first understand them in context of their knowledge, skills, and attitude. This helps to identify how they fit with the organization's needs; and see how we can support them to reach their potential. This does not mean that we are blind to their limitations and faults. We have to seek to understand their capacities in order to enable them to perform better. The essential role of a smart leader is to draw out the best in their people. Leaders must be able to discern enough in order to believe in people's potential and unlock that potential.

> *"The secret to success is good leadership, and good leadership is all about making the lives of your team members or workers better."* **- Tony Dungy**

Leaders play an important role in demonstrating conduct, compliance, considerations, shared responsibilities, and outcomes. They have to ensure not only better job performance but also influence general understanding and satisfaction of all in the organization. They are the role models for others, hence they are supposed to manage themselves by adjusting to the changing environment, think strategically in taking right decisions, and sustain relationship with all stakeholders to achieve organizational goals & objectives.

"Leadership competency is a set of visible essentials of managing self in adapting to the organizational behavior, thinking strategically for collaborative relationships to achieve results."- **Sanjay Bhattacharya, PhD**

Hence, competency entails following elements in leadership:

1. **Self- management-** Getting people to work together is not easy, and unfortunately many leaders skip over the basics of team building in a rush to start achieving goals. But our actions in the first few weeks and months can be to build people to deliver results and ultimately create a major impact. A leader must be able to demonstrate ethics and integrity while performing their job, being aware of self. They have an accurate picture of the value they can pass on to others smartly.

   "The key to successful leadership today is influence, not authority."- **Ken Blanchard**

   When leading others, they communicate effectively and value the diversity. They also smartly build interpersonal relationships, and develop others in managing teams/ group.

2. **Adaptability-** A leader should clearly understand the organization mission, vision, values, and strategy; to communicate and implement plan. People want to work toward something they believe in, so it is important that they buy in and work towards the same direction where the leader leads. If there is lack of clear understanding of the mission, goals, and vision by the leader, then there will not be a consistency in establishing work expectations and giving constructive feedback, in leading people. Therefore, the people should know exactly what they are working for, to give their best effort. Smart leader must be adaptable to the functions & goals of the entire business of the organization.

"Leadership is about vision and responsibility, not power." **- Seth Berkley**

Competent leaders have learning agility, and mentor /coach others from their experience and the opportunities that they are exposed to. A good leader is not one that has made no mistakes, but when they have made mistakes, they learn from them and find ways to prevent themselves from making the same mistake again.

3. **Strategic thinking-** Leaders who provide their team with a definite sense of direction and purpose paint a clear perspective between the overall picture and the details of day-to-day activities. Competent leaders think strategically about the identification of critical tasks and ably describe what success looks like. They constantly reinforce where the organization is heading and take key measures that lead to success in a smart manner. The people also need to see how their hard work makes a difference, and how it helps get the organization closer to achieving success.

"Sometimes leadership is planting trees under whose shade you'll never sit. It may not happen fully till after I'm gone. But I know that the steps we're taking are the right steps."- **Jennifer Granholm**

The leader should be able to smartly balance tension that occurs between strategic actions and daily tasks that will have a long-term impact on the organization. The term leading refers to the ability to solve problems, make decisions, manage changes, influence others, manage politics, innovate, take calculated risks, set the directions & strategies, etc.; of the business. Strategic thought pattern helps to construct a positive mindset that impact our performance. Strategic leadership calls for fully analyzing situation, understanding the potential impacts of each possible decision, and anticipating the outcomes of each decision.

4. **Collaborative relationships** – Leaders must have higher levels of engagement with different cross functional teams as these relationships helps to work together sharing the responsibility of reaching their goals together. Collaborative relationships mean that the process of decision-making is truly collective. In collaborative relationships, the end result is worked out among all the stakeholders who are the part of the decisions. Competent leaders ensure increased productivity through better-quality work and collaborative relationships.

> *"I don't know what leadership is. You can't touch it. You can't feel it. It's not tangible. But I do know this: you recognize it when you see it."* **- Bob Ehrlich**

Strong interpersonal skills promote communication and contribute to the overall morale of a team or group. Leaders must know to smartly build relationships between members of the team or group within the organization itself. Collaborative relationships foster trust between the members of the team or groups and promote a good enabling work environment. Leaders must be able to facilitate positive working relationships between multiple people respecting diversity and cross cultural dynamics when working together. Leaders with collaborative relationships listen actively when people express feelings and acknowledge their concerns. This makes the team members feel heard, improve their morale, create an environment of excitement, and encourage the development of more meaningful relationships.

5. **Achieving results-** Organization, team, or group is comprised of individuals with different talents and strengths. Evaluating and shaping high potential people in the organization, team, or group to deliver results by building their capacity promote a feeling of fairness among them who may wish to be considered for advancement as well. Leaders are expected to produce positive results for the organization from the team or group they lead. They do this by achieving their goals and objectives while leading their team or group to do the same. Effective leaders smartly focus on the competencies that lead to achieve results. They align with the people, process, system, structure, skills, culture, and values — to realize their strategies and desired outcomes. Competent leaders take corrective timely action with perfect plans to achieve results.

"Ultimately, leadership is not about glorious crowning acts. It is about keeping your team focused on a goal and motivated to do their best to achieve it, especially when the stakes are high and the consequences really matter. It is about laying the groundwork for others' success, and then standing back and letting them shine." **- Chris Hadfield**

A leader must continue to develop expertise, and continue to maintain high standard of accountability of available resources. They should utilize the resources properly to accomplish the necessary objectives, and assign accountability for those goals. The competent leader sets goals that include greater direction, greater focus, increased productivity, and higher levels of motivation. This leads to their daily actions to achieve results. They motivate others to achieve their personal best and value their contributions. Also, it is necessary for competent leaders to continue learning, as well as study competitors, to ensure that their knowledge and expertise will continue to grow as business changes.

Conclusion

We know that leadership is an important part of an organization's future. Identifying individuals with high potential for leadership is considered essential for producing future leaders in an organization.

"To educate a man in mind and not in morals is to educate a menace to society"
- Theodore Roosevelt

Leadership competencies are important part of shaping those individuals who have the higher potential to become influential leaders in the organization. By focusing on development of leadership competencies, an organization promote better leadership and also able to build future leaders from their current workforce to lead smartly.

Reflection:

- Evaluate your leadership competency in each of the five elements (self-management, adaptability, strategic thinking, collaborative relationship, and achieving results) mentioned and firm up your response to the stated questions:

Use the tool below-

i. How does my knowledge, skills, and attitude impact the way I lead?
ii. When did I sense the need to improve on the elements of my leadership competency?
iii. In what elements of leadership competency do I feel inadequate?
iv. What specifically can I do to improve my inadequacy in these element of leadership competency?
v. How do I want those under my authority to view my leadership?

- **Leadership Competency exercise**

Here is the list of few practices for each element of leadership competency. You may add more to the list. Quickly read through the list and place a tick (√) mark by those practices that you need to do for improving your leadership competency:

Element of Self-Management	Element of Adaptability	Element of Strategic Thinking	Element of Collaborative Relationships	Element of Achieving Results
Ethics in work	Demonstrate maturity	Demonstrate problem solving	Foster trust between the members of the team / group	Supporting individuals and teams in goal setting
Demonstrate integrity	Deep sense of commitment	Decision making	Promote a good work environment	Developing capacity
Self-awareness	Understand mission, vision, values of the organization	Change management	Respect diversity	Measuring performance
Value diversity	Committed to lifelong learning	Influence others	Actively managing cross-cultural dynamics between individuals/team/groups	Recognizing results
Maintain interpersonal relationships	Openness to both being mentored and mentoring and/or coaching others	Manage politics		
Develop others in managing teams / groups		Promote innovation		
		Take responsible risks		
		Set directions & strategies of the business		
		Analyze situations		
		Understand the potential impacts of each possible decision		
		Anticipate the outcomes of each decision		

- What steps could you take to improve the identified practice under each element of leadership competency? When will you do this? *Use this tool below:*

\multicolumn{5}{c}{Improvement Practice and Action Plan}
Sl. No.	Elements of Leadership Competency	Identified Practice for Improvement	Action Steps	By When
1	Self-Management			
2	Adaptability			
3	Strategic Thinking			
4	Collaborative Relationships			
5	Achieving Results			

Case Analysis

Developing Competencies for Leadership

Introduction

ABC is a not for profit organization that provides assistance to children and families. The Head- Evidence & Learning in ABC focuses on evaluating the skill-building programs. She reports directly to the ABC leadership. As a whole, the ABC has been cautious in hiring this year because of increased competition for federal grant funding. However, they have also suffered high staff turnover. Two directors, three key research staff, and one staff from the finance department have left. Head- Evidence & Learning has a demanding schedule that requires frequent travel; however, she being the Head of the Department (HoD); supervises two managers who in turn are responsible for five staff members each.

Issue

Both managers (1&2) have been appointed within the last six months.

Manager 1, has a specific background in research. She manages staff who provide research support to another department that delivers behavioral health services to youth. She supports her staff and is very organized; however, she often takes a very black and white view of issues. Upper level leadership values her latest research on the therapeutic division's services. She is very much motivated and driven; and expects the same from her staff.

Manager 2, has a strong background in social science research and evaluation. She manages staff that work on different projects within the ABC. She is known as a problem solver and is extremely supportive of her staff. She is very organized and has a wealth of experience in evaluation of family services. She is very much capable and can sometimes take on too much.

The managers are sensing that staff are becoming overworked as everyone takes on increased responsibilities due to high staff turnover. Staff have also mentioned that HoD's "glass half-empty" conversation style leaves them feeling dejected. In addition, HoD has not shared budgets with her managers, so they are having difficulty in appropriately allocating work to staff. HoD said that, she has not received sufficient information from the finance department to complete the budgets. The finance department said that, they have sent her all the information available with them.

Impact

As staff become distressed, the managers are becoming frustrated. They feel like they are unable to advocate for their staff or solve problems without key information like the departmental budget.

Discussion

1. How would you rate in (1-5) scale, where 1 being the lowest and 5 being the highest, for HoD's leadership competency elements i.e; self-management/adaptability/strategic thinking/collaborative relationships/ achieving results? And why?

Use this tool below:

\	Assessment of Elements of Leadership Competency		
Sl. No	Elements of Leadership Competency	Rating (1-5)	Reason
1	Self-Management		
2	Adaptability		
3	Strategic Thinking		
4	Collaborative Relationships		
5	Achieving Results		

2. What specific advice do you specially have for a leader to be effective in this situation?

LEADERSHIP TAKEAWAY

References:

1. ***Sevy, Bruce:*** *Identifying Competencies That Matter, leadership assessment products for PDI Ninth House.*
2. ***Zwell:*** *Creating a Performance Culture), the Art and Science of Competency Models.*

"You must accept responsibility for your actions, but not the credit for your achievements." - Denis Waitley

Chapter 4

Leading by Commitment

Introduction

Commitment is dedication to a particular cause, or belief, and a willingness to get involved. Committed people truly believe in what they do, create impact, and generate positive results. Commitment is needed before success can be experienced. It is often a person's heart that makes the difference between a good and a great leader. If we really want to make a difference in the life of others we need to look into our heart to see if we are really committed. The commitment to do what it takes to lead effectively comes with focus and a lot of hard work. It does not happen overnight; it starts with the decision, and continues with focus and perseverance. It is important to understand how others perceive us as a leader. Knowing where we stand, though potentially aching, is the first step to significantly changing the trajectory of our leadership. The leaders cannot wait for everything to be perfect before they are willing to commit themselves.

> *"We make a living by what we get, but we make a life by what we give."*
> *- Winston Churchill*

When there is commitment in the leader, a team, or group; people will buy into the leader before they buy into the vision. Commitment is a heart issue. Ken Blanchard said, "There's a difference between interest and commitment. When you are interested in doing something, you do it only when circumstances permit. When you are committed to something, you accept no excuses, only results." Commitment ignites action. Without it, people will not follow us.

Discussion questions:

1. What do you need to do to clarify your purpose to those around you?
   _____
   _____
   _____

2. Do you find your commitment in providing answers to people's questions? In what way does that impact your leadership?
   _____
   _____
   _____

3. Are you clearly able to align yourself to the mission, vision, and core values of the organization where you lead? Do others understand your leadership action? In what way can you improve in this area?
   _____
   _____
   _____

4. How does your leadership commitment shape your daily activities and choices? What are the current 'distractions' that you are facing which would take you away from your commitment?
   _____
   _____
   _____

5. Think of a committed leader you know who has demonstrated persistence, influence, and accomplished goals? How it has shaped your own view of commitment in leadership role?
   _____
   _____
   _____

6. What do you need to change to have that commitment?

_____
_____
_____

Forms of Leadership Commitment

Commitment is what keeps us going in the face of hardship and challenges. Commitment gives strength in our leadership as it is the backbone of a team or organization. If people are committed to an effort for a period of time, they learn from their mistakes and figure out a strategy that works to be more effective.

> *"Be slow to fall into friendship; but when thou art in, continue firm & constant."-Socrates*

Leaders need to continually evaluate their commitment to - their purpose, people they lead, and the organization they work. When we commit to the purpose that are truly important to us, we work alongside with our people who deliver results for the organization we serve. As our relationships improves, we will be more successful in achieving our goals. This helps to have more time to enjoy our journey of life. Our commitment does not end with the decisions.

Commitment is a leadership quality that inspires and attracts others. It shows that the leader has convictions and that the leader believes in the cause. There can be three forms of commitments for the leaders which are discussed as under:

1. **Commitment to the purpose** - Our leadership purpose is a statement about who we are as a person with values which are important to us and how we bring those unique qualities into our leadership to excel as a leader. Leadership purpose gives a better sense of purpose fit to be more satisfied in our work. This in turn

gives increased commitment. A clear purpose of the leader gives a clear vision with full integrity to the individuals and teams in the organization.

"The supreme quality for leadership is unquestionably integrity. Without it, no real success is possible, no matter whether it is on a section gang, a football field, in an army, or in an office."- **Dwight D. Eisenhower**

The leader with a purpose- help people reach their goals, leverage the talents of others, and take pride in the accomplishments. Using the people perspective, the goal of leadership is to bring out the best in people through respect, care, and continual support for their success. Key attributes of leadership purpose are to grow, to be bigger, stronger, and take responsible risks. They provide clarity of purpose motivating and guiding the people, team, and the organization to realize the mission.

2. **Commitment to the people-** Commitment is about the dedication of the leader to the organization, cause, or belief; and a willingness to get involved. The leadership commitment influence people in the organization for the effort they truly believe to be important; and they demonstrate it, follow through, and stick with it. Nothing worthwhile can be achieved without commitment. Commitment is tested by action. The real test of a leader's commitment is action and not mere talk. They need to work alongside with the people as partner in their performance.

"Leadership is about being a servant first."- **Allen West**

Since leadership is about influence, the leaders need to be committed to the people in terms of - recruiting and inducting new people as team members, providing quality training, and personalized development programs. This prepare people to deal with the challenges they face both currently and in the future. Leadership commitment to people enables to ensure that people's objectives and performance are perfectly aligned to those of the business. Commitment to people opens the door to achievement, and overcome obstacles / opposition. There will be times where their commitment to people is the only thing that carries them through to press on and get up no matter how many times they get knocked down.

3. **Commitment to the organization-** Leaders are the face of the organization to those they lead. If we as a leader want people to understand the mission and purpose of our organization, we need to invest our time, talent, and heart into the work. We must be able to communicate the mission and purpose of the organization clearly, but it is far more important that people see us living it first.

> *"No institution can possibly survive if it needs geniuses or supermen to manage it. It must be organized in such a way as to be able to get along under a leadership composed of average human beings."* **- Peter Drucker**

As always, people watch our feet, more than our lips. If we want more commitment from our team members, start with ourselves. When the leaders are committed to the organization's vision, they are able to communicate that vision to people. They develop the connection or bond with the people in the organization. It shows that the leader has convictions and that the leader believes in the cause. A team will value the team leader and subsequently improve the people engagement in terms of - organizational change, performance, people satisfaction, working toward organization's success, and focusing on achieving goals. Thus the influence of the values of the organization becomes visible.

Elements of Commitment in Leadership

People who are committed set examples for others and tends to overcome hindrances as they do not give up and hold out for the rewards of success. The commitment effectively influences others because of determination and, people pay attention to it. Leadership commitment fosters people, team, or organization to keep going for accomplishing the set goals.

"The function of leadership is to produce more leaders, not more followers."-
Ralph Nader

Leadership commitment is about - demonstration of continuous persistence by self, shape influence on others, and craving for accomplishment of goals.

A committed leader continues moving forward, looking for solutions, and working toward success. This persistent quality confronts challenges and retain our perspective even when the challenges of leadership become stressful or complicated. It can take years to become successful, with persistence playing a vital role in the process.

An effective leader moves followers into action not with coercion but by eliciting their desire and articulating conviction in the vision & goals. When we commit to the people and things that are truly important to us, our career, or our organization; the results are that - our relationships with people will improve, we will be more successful in achieving our goals, and we will have more time to enjoy our journey.

Leadership commitment plays an important role for the achievement of the goals. Commitment urges us gradually to explore ourselves because it is a source to transform a capacity into a reality. The belief in our inner self is the foundation of commitment that makes us closer to the accomplishment of goal. Commitment is an intelligent emotional bond of accomplishment.

> *"Commitment in leadership is uninterrupted persistence by the leader that build influence on others for accomplishment of goals."-* ***Sanjay Bhattacharya, PhD***

Hence commitment entails the following elements in leadership:

1. **Continuous persistence-** Committed leaders are persistent towards their goal or vision that keeps them driving for a higher purpose.

They are deeply ingrained to focus on their goal or vision constantly with great emotion and energy. They relentlessly pursue goals even when the challenges of leadership get tough, stressful, or complicated.

"Commitment requires hard work in the heat of the day; it requires faithful exertion in behalf of chosen purposes and the enhancement of chosen values."- John Gardner

Commitment in leadership calls for persistence which is the ability to continue moving forward, looking for solutions, and working toward success. There may be challenges to peruse our goals or vision but as a leader - we need to improve with our failures and learn from those experiences to move on, having enough determination to go on, and not give up. Persistence as part of our leadership commitment, keeps us pushing through to complete a project and become really smart at something when others give it away.

2. **Build influence-** Influencing skills are the ability to bring people round to our way of thinking about a certain task with common understanding, without force or coercion whilst acknowledging their opinions. Committed leaders are able to influence others by their hard work, out of loyalty. They have a unique endurance that allows them to keep going because they are mentally wired to work endlessly toward their dreams. Commitment in any organization directly influence all. Leadership has been described as the ability to influence others. The commitment does not end with the decision. They smartly make more disciplined and productive decisions, and are more willing to go out of the comfort zone.

"Take chances, make mistakes. That's how you grow. Pain nourishes your courage. You have to fail in order to practice being brave."
– Mary Tyler Moore

Committed leaders has to show respect to others because they are loyal and will give something of value (time, money, effort) to support each other in achieving the common goal or vision. They need to keep promises and protect teammates from harm even when it is hard to do so. The stronger our commitment, the more likely we are able to influence others to succeed as we refuse to give up or give in.

3. **Accomplish goals** - Leaders who are committed truly believe that it is important to achieve the goals. Committed people constantly make new goals or vision and are always determined to push their boundaries and achieve more. They demonstrate the ways, follow through, and stick with it. Commitment is needed in every walk of leadership and it is the fundamental source which leads us towards our destinations or goals.

> *"The biggest differentiator of companies that excel in leadership development is the commitment and ownership of the CEO or top executive."* — **Dan McCarthy**

Leadership commitment has an important role for making incremental progress towards accomplishing a great goal. They smartly chose a clear goal, make plans, and focus to achieve it. This helps to ensure the road map of our goal. They ignite the passion to consistently equip others with new experiences. Commitment is a means that is required for every leader to be successful.

Committed leaders think about each person as a potential leader and build their capability to lead in order to sustain commitment of people in the team or organization. This further helps in continuous persistence, build influence, and accomplish goals. If people view themselves as a leader of a group, they will own the group as theirs, as they will have a feeling of ownership and will be more likely to take initiative to make sure things work well.

Conclusion

Commitment is dedication to purpose, people, or organization; and a willingness to get involved in the cause or belief.

"Leadership development is a life time journey, not a brief trip." **-John Maxwell**

Leadership commitment is not easy and at times there may be personal consequences when leading an unpopular change. However, leadership commitment is what separates true leaders from people in positions of leadership. The committed leaders thrive in their efforts and impact people to work together in coordination to reach the destination in a smart manner. More holistically, they are responsible for making the needed resources available along with people growth and development because it is about the direction they set in leading people towards destination.

Reflection:

- Deliberate on the way to improve on the elements of committed leadership.
- State three action steps you would like to take for yourself in each element.

Use this tool below:

Element of committed leadership	Action step 1	Action step 2	Action step 3
Continuous persistence			
Build influence			
Accomplish goals			

Case Analysis

Leadership Commitment to Change

Introduction

ABC is a large manufacturing industry and the senior leadership was concerned about their high accident frequency and severity rates. They wanted to address the issues arising out of accidents and be best in class for their industry. It had an effect on the productivity of the organization.

Issue

ABC had a traditional way of working in the manufacturing process for long time and due to high accident frequency the leadership was committed to change the safety culture in the organization.

Action

In order to bring about a cultural change in the safety of the people in the organization following measures were taken:

1- *Assessment:* Specific tools were used in the assessment process and it included-
   - Assess the current safety culture, including attitudes, and beliefs.
   - Understanding current leadership approaches and what they focus on, particularly front-line leaders.
   - Learn the current systems and practices used while working.
   - Review the training that has been conducted for developing competence.
   - Review the forms and documents for reporting and how often they are used.

- Understand the method of accident investigation, teaching lessons learned, and the follow up.
- Interview team leaders and managers; conducting focus group discussions with employees about issues surrounding higher rate of accidents.
- Conduct change readiness assessment.

Outcome of the Assessment - The assessment uncovered a fairly comprehensive list of items that would contribute to a lower view of their safety culture. The attitude and belief that production is much more important was by far the most glaring concern. Team members did not feel they could take the time that was required of them to perform their tasks safely and if they did there would likely be some kind of performance discussion.

2- *Senior Management workshop:* A senior manager workshop was conducted where there was discussion on the assessment report and subsequently planning the projects and actions to build a safety culture. It was believed that the management team would see the plan they developed to change the safety culture through to completion. By the nature of the projects and timelines given, it was pretty clear it would take some time to reach best-in-class for their industry.

3- *First Manager Review meeting:* After working on the plan for a while, the first management review meeting was held to discuss what had been accomplished. At that meeting it was obvious- the team was tense, and eventually they said the change was taking a lot of effort. They did not see the accident frequency and severity rates decreasing fast enough. The senior team had neglected to say in the planning meetings that they had promised their shareholder to be best-in-class for accident severity rates and frequency rates for their industry within a year.

It was agreed that the current plan to address the safety culture would take longer than a year to have the level of impact they were looking for, particularly since some of the first parts of the plan were meant to address leadership approaches, and the practices seemed to put production first over safe production. They believed these items laid a solid foundation for all the other changes. It was mutually decided to not continue the project together.

They decided to change the broader safety culture plan and target the incidents that happened the most over the last year. This activity was in the plan but it was not considered to be the primary action to change the safety culture. They held a series of 'behavior change communication' campaigns with staff about the most common types of incidents. They hoped targeting those incidents would create enough awareness to reduce their accident frequency and severity rate quick enough to satisfy their shareholders.

Impact

It was finally decided that, in almost every safety culture initiative; ABC shall be the part of building awareness about the most common issues, but it is not the only action to change the whole culture.

Although ABC started with the right intent to assess and understand what was causative to their current safety culture, they felt they could quickly change without taking all the necessary steps.

Changing safety culture takes time, energy, and a real passion from everyone involved; but particularly by senior leaders - leading by example to work on changing the foundation of how the organization runs.

Conclusion

It may sound like this case was a failure, but during the interrogation of the project, ABC came to understand that they had incorrectly assumed that they had the passion for the overall culture change. They missed checking that everyone at the senior management level had the willingness to commit to the effort and the time it would take. Knowing what to do did not translate into a willingness to do it and in the end, the desire to get the result quickly outweighed the desire to really change the safety culture.

Safe work cultures do everything they can to ensure that production never comes before ensuring everyone goes home safe and healthy every day.

Discussion

Discourse your observations on elements of the ABC's leadership commitment to change its safety culture.

Use this tool below:

Elements of Leadership commitment	What went well?	What did not go well?	Recommendations
Continuous persistence			
Build influence			
Accomplish goals			

LEADERSHIP TAKEAWAY

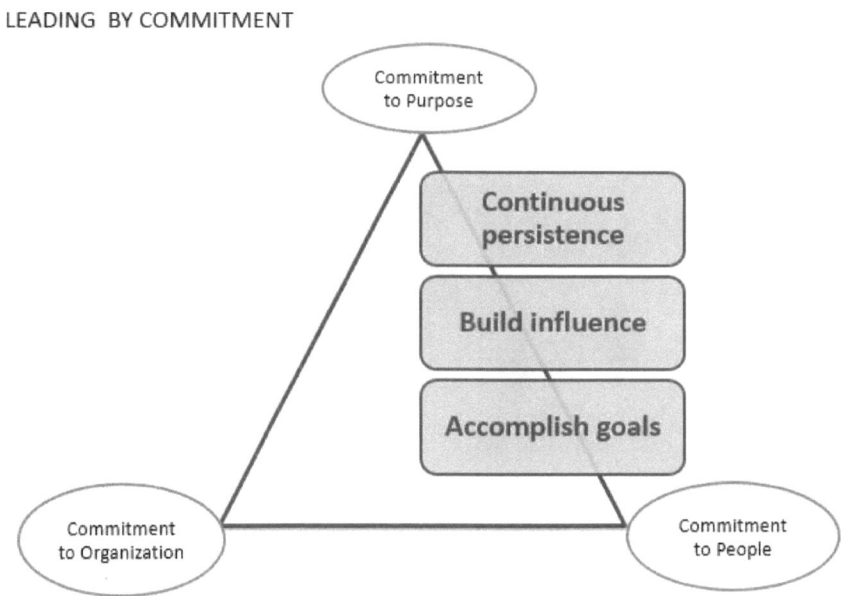

References:

1. **Hopkin, Michael Ray**: *How to lead with commitment;* https://leadonpurposeblog.com/2017/03/27/how-to-lead-with-commitment/, (March 27, 2017).

2. **Beike, Scott** : *Leadership Commitment;* https://brightonleadership.com/leadership-commitment/(September 27, 2011).

"Nothing splendid has ever been achieved except by those who dared believe that something inside of them was superior to circumstance."- Bruce Barton

Chapter 5

Leading by Confidence

Introduction

People look to the leader's reaction and for the answers when situation go wrong. They need to be confident in their leadership skills. It is important to be always calm, and be the example as a confident leader, even if the organization is experiencing a major decline. The job of a leader is to maintain the pleasant work environment, and continue leading for addressing the challenges. Confident people are the ones who believe in her/his own abilities for accomplishments and efforts. Being confident not only helps us to seek new opportunities but also builds a trust in ourselves to perform.

Very few people succeed in life without a degree of confidence. Confidence comes from feelings of well-being, self-esteem, and belief in our own abilities, skills, & experience. In business setup, self-confidence is necessary for leaders to take responsible risks and accomplish high goals at all levels - individual, team, and organization. When a leader lacks confidence, the consequences affect the entire team. Unconfident leaders withhold information, postpone important decisions, have trouble building teams, and inspiring them. Without confidence, there is no leadership—because what we do not have, we cannot give to others.

> *"The only thing standing between you and your goal is the bullshit story you keep telling yourself as to why you can't achieve it."*- **Jordan Belfort**

Confidence levels are boosted by perseverance, practice, training, knowledge, and interacting with others. Confident leaders tend to deal immediately and directly with issues, rather than pro-casting, ignoring, or passing problems to others. Confidence in leadership is to remain true to themselves and their values with integrity as they take responsibility for moving ahead to achieve results. They are smart to handle crisis situation being visionaries, motivators, and encouragers.

Discussion questions:

1. How is confidence expressed in your leadership?
   _____
   _____

2. How have past experiences with leaders shaped your own confidence in your role?
   _____
   _____
   _____

3. In what ways do they encourage you to build confidence in leading your team?
   _____
   _____
   _____

4. Does your leadership most often build others up or tear them down? What examples can you give of how this has been demonstrated in the past?
   _____
   _____
   _____

5. How confident are you as a leader in the scale of 1-5 (where 1 being the lowest and 5 being the highest)? In what ways is this related to how you see your own capability? What do you need to change to have the confidence?
   _____
   _____
   _____

Elements of Confident Leadership

Confidence means feeling sure of ourselves and our abilities — not in an egotistical way, but in a genuine, safe way. It is not about feeling superior to others. Confident people feel secure because of their capabilities to perform and impact. Confident leaders envision positive outcomes no matter what the situation may be. They believe that they have the talent and abilities to lead through an issue for positively impacting the people, team, or organization. They generally tend to have a positive outlook on life, and they have a strong belief in themselves. This belief allows them to take responsible risks and persevere through failures while all the while believing that goals will happen eventually. They constantly shape and guide individuals while making right decisions to keep moving.

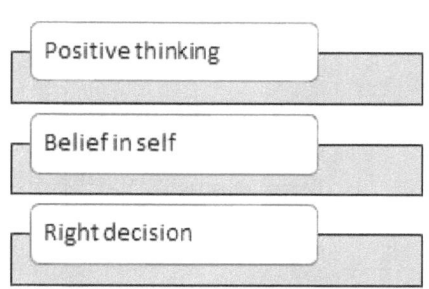

*"Confident leader think positively towards possible solutions of the concerns, believing in the ability of self, forecasting the expected outcomes in directing individuals towards right decisions."-**Sanjay Bhattacharya, PhD**.*

Hence confidence entails the following elements in leadership:

1. **Positive thinking –** A positive attitude helps to see the good in all things. In positive thinking, our approach to unpleasantness is to stay productive. Positive thinking stream of unspoken thoughts that run through our mind- the best is going to happen as a result of our effort. It changes the way we look at situations to stay in control of our approach of moving ahead in difficult situations, no matter how bad they may seem to be. A positive mind-set is an important skill we can develop in ourselves.

    *"A life spent making mistakes is not only more honourable but more useful than a life spent doing nothing." - **George Bernard Shaw***

Positive action keeps us motivated in achieving the goals we set for ourselves through increased sense of confidence there by managing challenges better and learning from mistakes. The positivity in the leadership contributes to care for the people in the task accomplishment and optimistic approach. They are discussed as under:

- *Care for people-*Positive thinking in the leaders help them to look for the good in people they lead because they want to see the best from them. They display that, they are confident in the ability of the people they lead to put their best foot forward to accomplish the task. Confident leaders understand that they need oneness in the effort and work as partner with them, rallying behind them straight to the finish line.

- *Optimistic approach-* Positive thinking leads to optimism that can go a long way to improving the path way of circumstances. A positive attitude can help leaders to put everything into perspective and asses the circumstances for the way forward plans. It is important to understand what we can control and change, and what we cannot. Being optimistic builds our confidence and gives us the motivation to move past any stressful situation and lead people towards achieving the goals.

2. **Belief in self-** Considering ourselves to be capable of success increases our chances of actual success. Belief in self means having faith in our own capabilities. It is a 'can do' attitude within our self which is crucial to succeed in goal setting, completing the task, and achieving the set goals.

"Where hope grows, miracles blossom."- Elna Rae

A confident leader believes in self about the ability of the team or group for the future course of action and is willing to take the responsible risks necessary to achieve their personal and professional goals. This is the attitude about their people skills and abilities. It means that they trust themselves as well as the people they lead and have a sense of control in their life. They are discussed as under:

- *Trust-* Belief in self leads to affirmative view of oneself knowing the strengths and weakness of individual, group or team, very well; to have a constructive view of being a confident leader.
- *Sense of control-* Self-control behaviour is significant for believing in self. Confident leaders assume the ability to take action, be effective, influence their own life, and assume responsibility for their behaviours in decision making of all scenarios. Sense of control is the extent to which people believe that they have power over events in their lives. It set realistic expectations & goals, communicate assertively, and handle criticism.

3. **Right decision-** As a leader we need to make right choices in arriving at the decisions which are precise, and ethical in standards. Making right decisions leads to right results with more options and flexibility with opening up for new opportunities. When we make right decisions, it also means we are learning from our mistakes.

> *"I quit being afraid when my first venture failed and the sky didn't fall down."- Allen H. Neuharth*

A confident leader enters into the right decision-making process with an open mind and do not let their own biases influence them. Right decision requires an original viewpoint and validated information. They are discussed as under:

- *Original viewpoint-* A good decision might open up a new opportunity by shutting off other options. When we make right decisions, it also means we are learning from our mistakes by exploring the original view point that helps the leader to be confident. This further helps to choose actions that gives the best outcome for the individual, team or group; and gain a new perspective.

- *Validated information-* The decision-making process by confident leaders requires that they maintain clarity of information and see all choices as valid until they eliminate the options later. A leader with confident decision making skills will seek data to validate accuracy of information and relevancy in potential solutions. They combine experience and perception, with information to find the best solution. They make decisions rationally, after researching alternatives and understanding the consequences.

Confidence is one of the most important leadership traits in achieving success. Confidence is a state of mind that comes from- our positive thinking, belief in self, and taking the right decisions. It is an essential expertise of a smart leader to develop others and attain high levels of achievement.

Conclusion

Confidence helps us feel ready for life's experiences. When we are confident, we are more likely to move forward with people and take opportunities rather than back away from them. And if things do not work out initially, confidence helps us to attempt again. On the other hand, when a leader lacks confidence, the consequences affect the entire team. The leaders who are not confident hide facts, delay key decisions, and are unable to motivate teams. They fail to build other because of their inability to give the needed enhancement opportunities to the people as they lack leadership expertise.

> *"Don't let the incidents which take place in life brings you low. And certainly don't whine. You can be brought low, that's OK, but don't be reduced by them. Just say, 'that's life'."* - **Maya Angelou**

The confident leaders are smart in observing things carefully, analysis the course of action for success, and learn for the past mistakes of self as well as others. Therefore, they visualize constructive results no matter what the circumstances may be, to impact their organization positively.

They believe in themselves and the people to overcome any issue. Confident leaders are meticulously smart in taking the right steps leading to achievement.

Reflection:

- Evaluate your leadership confidence in each of the three elements (positive thinking, belief in self, and right decision) mentioned and firm up your response to the stated questions:

Use the tool below-

Elements of Leadership Confidence	Question	Response
Positive thinking	How do I recognize seeing good in the people even in bad situations to get the best from them, in my leadership?	
	How do I have to influence people by putting everything into viewpoint and asses the circumstances for the way forward?	
Belief in self	How do I tend to be affirmative on the strengths and weakness of individuals, group or team?	
	How do I set realistic expectations and goals, communicate assertively, and handle criticism in my leadership?	
Right decision	How have my leadership experiences and the thinking of those around me shaped my view of exploring the original view point to choose actions that give the best outcome?	
	In what ways do you maintain clarity of information and see all choices as valid?	

- What steps could you take to improve your leadership confidence? And when will you do this?

Use this tool below:

	Improvement Areas and Action Plan			
Sl. No.	Leadership Confidence	Improvement Area	Action steps	By When
1	Positive Thinking			
2	Belief in Self			
3	Right Decision			

Case Analysis

Gaining Confidence for New Leadership Role

Introduction

A Director started in her new role at a prominent national level organization ABC and seemed to define her personal brand and leadership style. She focused on building and expanding her team, reacting in real-time to fluid situations and finding the confidence to assert herself with senior leadership of ABC.

Issue

As a person in the new role she is unfamiliar with the senior leadership team of ABC. The organization was changing and she saw an opportunity to help her define that shift — and develop her own unique professional presence. She needed coaching and guidance on how to build a high functioning team while also developing her personal leadership style and gaining confidence to function at more of an executive level.

Action

In order to achieve her goal, she decided for making her move to have a guidance from somebody who can coach her. She needed someone who could help her hold space for that vision of the future while responding in real-time to the situation on the ground. Subsequently she followed up with the leadership development team of ABC, sharing her need and began what ended up in getting a coaching engagement with the concerned person in leadership development team. Both met for regular one-on-one coaching sessions to discuss roadblocks and map out strategies that would help her make progress in developing confidence.

A lot of the sessions really grounded her well to apply it directly to what she wanted to be doing. These sessions helped her- to think positively with concern for the people whom she is leading and have optimistic approach in her leadership style; to have belief in herself and her people, having a constructive view of self-control over the events, and to take right decisions with original viewpoint through validated information.

Impact

They were kind of like 'aha' moments, where she was able to suddenly see the problems differently. The sessions felt healing in as way, because she was able to come out of her barriers of confidence and apply what she learned right away. The biggest impact for her has been a sense of peace in her days and confidence in using her voice within the team and the organization.

One of her biggest takeaways in working on her leadership style and presence within the organization has been her newfound sense of confidence. She was a lot more confident than before.

She said, "Our work has given me the confidence to walk into those meetings with senior executives of ABC and have the sense of building my confidence."

Discussion

1. What steps are taken by the Director in her new role in ABC to build her confidence?
2. What worked well for her in developing her leadership confidence?

LEADERSHIP TAKEAWAY

LEADING BY CONFIDENCE

References:

1. **Bonds, Regina:** *Five signs you're leading with confidence*, Chief Executive Insights, CEOWORLD Magazine; March 2022.

2. **McCarthy, Dan:** *12 ways to develop leadership confidence*, Blog Great Leadership, www.greatleadershipbydan.com, 2015.

"Kindness is the language which the deaf can hear and the blind can see."- Mark Twain

Chapter 6

Leading by Compassion

Introduction

Compassion is often regarded as having sensitivity, willingness, and desire to be kind to others. It means being thoughtful and aware of what others' lives and experiences are like. Compassion motivates people to go out of their way to help the physical, mental, or emotional pains of others.

Compassion is not something we are born with, but it grows out of considerate behavior. If we want to complement our leadership with heart-based qualities like compassion, then we must remember that our heart is a muscle, and muscles require exercise. Therefore, if we want to become more compassionate, we need to intentionally practice it. It may not seem natural, but the more we work on our compassion, the more it will become natural to us.

Compassion profoundly shapes the way we lead. It is essential for productivity, people happiness, and the work environment. When mistakes are made, even if they are serious; it is important to look at the bright side of things, though it would be easy to get upset and lash out. We are setting the tone for the work day, and our attitude directly affects those under our leadership. Act of compassion can have a significant impact on their work day and those to come.

"The truest greatness lies in being kind; the truest wisdom is a happy mind."
*- **Ella Wheeler Wilcox***

Compassionate leadership recognizes that every team member is unique and also an essential thread in the fabric of an entire organization. They strive to enhance the happiness and well-being of their people by supporting them with what they need to excel. Compassionate leadership is focused on what is best for the individual, the team, and the organization in the long-term. Today, leaders are expected to treat their people with a greater sense of care and humanity to respect the unique attributes and qualities each person bring to the team and organization. They do not use shame to control behavior in others.

Discussion questions:

1. Whom do you see as the one who lead with compassion? What has shaped him/herself to be a compassionate leader?
   _____
   _____

2. When those who follow me make mistakes, what is my default response? Does it reflect compassion? Am I able to treat others when they make mistakes like the way I want to be treated when I make mistakes?
   _____
   _____
   _____

3. Would my followers describe me as a leader "full of compassion"? Why or why not? What can I do to become more compassionate?
   _____
   _____
   _____

Behaviours of Compassionate Leaders

There are many traits leaders must have in order to successfully lead. One trait that may be just as important is compassion; which translates into empathy and concern for individuals, teams, and the organization.

> *"Life is 10% of what happens to me and 90% of how I react to it."*
> **- John Maxwell**

Compassionate leadership helps others to move forward because it is a combination of empathy, and good leadership skills. They understand that their employees are people before being employees, and people have needs. They take time out to check in with the team members individually to make sure they are doing well personally as well as professionally. Generally, people who are compassionate are more satisfied with their lives, and enjoy stronger relationships. It helps other people, and make them feel good.

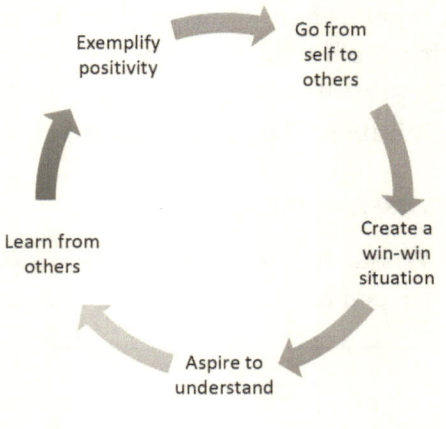

Compassion is fuelled by wanting to actually take action to help individuals, teams, and the organization. Here are five behaviors mentioned below, to have compassion in our leadership:

1. **Go from self to others-** Compassionate leaders understand that 'I' is not especially useful as a conversation starter, and that when leaders stop focusing on their own egos they are able to connect with others to develop them. The entire practice of compassion is about going from self to others, from 'I' to 'we'.

    *"Awards become corroded, friends gather no dust." **- Jesse Owens***

    Everyone feels important and warmly wanted in the team or organization, when leaders are open on accommodating others, because they have a good start and work together with collective goals. Compassionate leader show respect and give credit to others by listening to them in the team or organization. When the situation merits all enjoy the success.

2. **Create a win-win situation-** In a win-win negotiation, both the leader and followers are satisfied with their agreement, the chances of a long-lasting success are much higher.

   "Hope never abandons you, you abandon it."- **George Weinberg**

   Compassionate leaders hope to invest time with individuals, teams, and organization to yield great dividends of relationships, so that people experience a strong relationship with their leader. They give constructive criticism whenever required. Subsequently they are willing to offer their best to work out a win-win situation. A win-win situation is the result of a mutual-gains approach to negotiation in which parties work together to meet interests and maximize value creation.

3. **Aspire to understand-** Being compassionate is key to understanding others. When someone is reaching out to a compassionate leader, they take their hand, listen to them, and give them their time. In the workplace, people often work together in groups or teams which may be cross functional also. The skill of understanding others not only helps us predict what people might feel in a certain situation, but it also allows us to make sense of how people react in certain situation. Understanding others does not mean that we have to agree with their feelings or point of view. Instead, it means that we recognize their point of view, and accept that it is different from ours. Hence we agree to disagree with others.

   "Being strong means rejoicing in who you are, complete with imperfections."- **Margaret Woodhouse**

   Compassionate leaders have concern for everyone in spite of all differences. They excel at inviting people for shared vision and goals. They also help create the action steps needed to achieve them. This approach to understand individuals, teams, and organization helps in plugging the gaps in performance. It results in an environment where people feel good about themselves and own the task with commitment and doing it well.

4. **Learn from others-** When we are open to learning from others, we benefit from their experience as well and we receive their wisdom and knowledge. To gather or obtain specific knowledge, wisdom, or experience from some people who are different from us inspire us to do something- different, better, or more meaningful. This is also called as social learning, and it has to do with the people around us, i.e. we learn from others by watching and interacting with them. We can also learn by seeing someone else's mistakes to avoid falling into the same trap. Learning from others allows us to see and learn about different types of struggles people might have. This further helps to develop empathy, which is an important life skill.

"If you don't go after what you want, you'll never have it. If you don't ask, the answer is always no. If you don't step forward, you're always in the same place."- **Nora Roberts**

Compassionate leaders surround themselves with intelligent people who possess wisdom and are smart. Talents are leveraged by giving them the chance to contribute their expertise and strengths. Being stubborn or thinking we know it all kills compassion. Instead, there is a need of being open to learn from others when faced with a situation that might require more process-oriented thinking.

5. **Exemplify positivity-** People with positive outlook in life cope up better with stressful situation. Exemplifying the power of positive leadership help people feel more connected with the organization's purpose, vision, mission, values, and overall culture. People today want to feel a sense of belonging with shared values in the organization they work. Positive leadership is modeling, facilitating, and purposefully influencing positive emotions that encourage individuals and teams to excel in their work. Positive leaders nurture an enabling environment for physical and mental well-being of

people through communication, accountability, motivation, and work ethic.

"Holding on to anger, resentment and hurt only gives you tense muscles, a headache, and a sore jaw from clenching your teeth. Forgiveness gives you back the laughter and the lightness in your life." **- Joan Lunden**

Compassionate leaders are able to empower and motivate others by simply being a genuinely positive person. This helps to develop a positive mental attitude and be the kind of leader who always has something good to say and make people feel comfortable. They guide, acknowledge, and support others to combine their efforts, skills, talents, insights, passion, enthusiasm, and commitment to work together for the greater good. When compassion is present, defensiveness decreases and something positive replace it.

These practices of compassionate leadership keep the leader more grounded, productive, and successful. Being compassionate means taking the longer-term view and doing what is best for everyone. Therefore, the better thing to do is to respectfully and firmly offer constructive criticism, and be frank / straightforward to break the critical news. Then, the people can indeed learn, grow, and become more attuned to goals of individual, team, or the organization.

Exercise:

Think about all dynamics in your leadership, which can contribute to each of the five behaviors of compassion we discussed. Make a list of them against each behavior of compassion mentioned.

Use this tool below:

• Go from self to others	
• Create a win-win situation	
• Aspire to understand	
• Learn from others	
• Exemplify positivity	

Elements of Compassion in Leadership

Compassion has to do much more in our leadership style. It is about having the ability to relate to and connect with people for the purpose of motivating and empowering their lives. It means identifying ourselves with others and being mindful by seeing them as a part of themselves and relating to what they are experiencing at a much deeper level. Compassionate leader expresses recognition by listening to people. Subsequently they are gratified and cared through support, mentorship, and guidance. People feel inspired to accomplish great things for themselves, their team, or the organization. Compassionate leadership foster people to work together collectively because of what their leadership mean for the people.

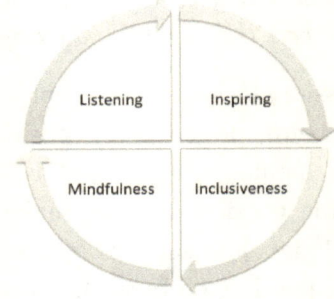

"Compassionate leadership is about being mindful of people and listen to their thoughts in order to inspire and inclusive for the greater good." - **Sanjay Bhattacharya, PhD.**

Hence compassion entails following elements in leadership:

1. **Mindfulness-** Leaders have to show the same care and consideration, as to themselves to the people they lead. They have to consciously cultivate their ability to be present with open-mind when interacting with their team members. It is also important for leaders to be mindful because it helps them to understand the expectations of those working under them with increased trust, satisfaction, and positive organizational culture. In compassion there is tremendous willingness to communicate with others more mindfully giving room for them to express themselves.

"It took me a long time not to judge myself through someone else's eyes."
- Sally Field

When leaders are mindful, they ask thoughtful questions to receive thoughtful answers. They also pay attention to body language and provide continuous meaningful feedback based on the thinking and behavioral preferences of team members. The compassionate leader is smart in seeking to understand people, knowing that understanding is the doorway for the greatest impact on guiding others. These leaders hold a deep concern for how their team members feel and what they are getting out of their work experience.

2. **Listening-** Listening is one of the most powerful tools for a leader. It builds trust, creates transparency, and foster loyalty. It lets others know that they are important and valued individuals. Unfortunately, many leaders are unaware of this fact and never learn how to effectively listen. Active listening also gives leaders insight about the stress and tension points of those they lead. It is the strong people engagement driver as it enhances the ability to understand individual better and encourages stronger communication between leaders and team members.

"When we meet anger with anger we can expect an explosion, but when anger meets love and kindness it loses its strength." **–Joyce Meyer**

Compassion helps in listening to others and make them feel important as an individual. In a team or organization, compassionate leaders get inputs by encouraging open discussion about work. By listening to others we succeed to support and guide those to stay focused. When people are heard, they start thinking in terms of success rather than failure. Leaders have the role of helping people through ways to remove any barriers they may face. Compassionate leaders smartly express themselves to be empathetic, sympathetic, and understanding- in other words, they are considerate; by listening to the concerns of the people. The people become comfortable in sharing their ideas and offering creative solutions, when they are listened. They derive a satisfaction of being heard.

3. **Inspiring-** There has to be a high level of trust and integrity in daily actions by the leaders to inspire people. Leaders have to show their willingness to put forth the same effort, being asked by others. Compassionate leaders inspire others by taking responsible risk to develop their team members and provide them with opportunities to succeed. They constantly influence others, by seeking inputs on important decisions that will affect them individually or the team as a whole. When the individuals are well connected with the leader through their involvement in the very early stage of implementing any changes, they are able to express themselves and understood by the leader.

"Success is not final, failure is not fatal, it is the courage to continue that counts." - ***Winston Churchill***

Leading requires the skill to ignite passion in others. When we treat people with compassion they never forget. These leaders ignite passion in others to approach every task they do, down to the smallest details, with determination. Compassionate leaders know smartly that - there is nothing more powerful than a person who are driven from their heart. Therefore, they lead from within, with the ability to inspire others through encouragement and empowerment.

4. **Inclusiveness-** Inclusion comprehends people's involvement and empowerment. People are at their best when they feel included. Inclusiveness in leadership occurs when leaders successfully understand what makes each individual in the team or organization unique, and also support them in bringing out the best in them. Inclusiveness promote diverse thinking and ensures that people are recognized, respected, heard, and valued.

*"As iron sharpens iron, so one man sharpens another." -**Proverbs 27:17***

Compassion lay the groundwork for others to have the best chance of success, and hold the wisdom that great things in life or business are never accomplished by one person. Compassionate leaders take great joy in watching team members shine individually and collectively. They guide their people to perform at a high level of excellence by creating a culturally inclusive framework where people work effectively across all functions for collective good. They smartly facilitate inclusive effort of all people in the ups or downs to their expectations and set the bar high on quality but keep it within reach. When quality is expected, inclusiveness naturally increases and allow people to experience the successes they have accomplished.

Compassionate leaders mindfully help others live with an attitude of abundance and prefer to look at what team members need rather than at what team members are not doing. It is important to note that compassionate leadership is all about giving people what they need and not necessarily what they want. Compassionate leadership seek influence, rather exercise authority. These leaders do not demand but they encourage people with listening to them. They do all they can to inspire team members to give nothing less than their best. They are more inclusive and create higher levels of overall people engagement by creating an environment where people feel a greater sense of commitment to their organization. They are smart to view challenges with interest and sets the tone for people to keep high morale.

Conclusion

Compassion begins with an inclination to see and feel the pulse of the people we lead and work on it keeping in mind their best interest. The actions of compassionate leaders smartly comprise of going from self to others to create a winning situation by aspiring to understand the people, learning from them, and creating positivity. A leader with compassion means being able to comprehend when a colleague is becoming overwhelmed and assigning someone to help them complete their tasks.

"Our life of poverty is as necessary as the work itself. Only in heaven will we see how much we owe to the poor for helping us to love God better because of them." **- Mother Teresa**

Compassion is our ability to know the feelings of others and act on them for healthier interactions. Compassionate leadership embodies a tangible expression of mindfulness, listening, inspiring, and inclusiveness for those we lead within the team or organization.

Reflection:

- Evaluate the strength of -Mindfulness, Listening, Inspiring, and Inclusiveness; elements of "Compassion", in your leadership role. Rate them in the scale of 1-10 in these elements of compassionate leadership. Would you say you are –

    i. Strong (If your score is 8-10)
    ii. Average (If your score is 6-7)
    iii. Weak (If your score is 1-5)

- What steps could you take to improve? (if your rating is average or weak)
- When will you do this?

Use this tool below:

Elements of Compassion in Leadership								
Mindfulness (Strong/Average/Weak)		Listening (Strong/Average/Weak)		Inspiring (Strong/Average/Weak)		Inclusiveness (Strong/Average/Weak)	
Rating=		Rating=		Rating=		Rating=	
Action Steps	By when	Action Steps	By when	Action Steps	By when	Action Steps	By when

Case Analysis

Compassion at Workplace

Introduction

ABC Hospital is an organization working in the healthcare sector. It is an agreeable fact that compassion is fundamental to patient care. The majority of the people in healthcare work hard to offer compassionate care to their patients. The mission of ABC Hospital is about providing quality healthcare and cherished experience, reinforced by a team of compassionate and dedicated medical professionals. The ABC Hospital was set up with this mission to fulfil its following strategic objectives:

- To be the center of excellence for medical care, research, and academics.
- To nurture an environment of trust, honesty, mutual respect, equality, and ethics.

It started off very well but over a period of time, ABC Hospital became one example where a lack of compassion led to people experiencing serious failings in basic standards of care, causing to suffering, and avoidable deaths.

Issues

The leadership team of ABC made an assessment of how compassion in the workplace looks like and then look at how compassionate workplaces might impact on staff, patients, and the overall organization. They identified following concerns in the current work environment:

1. *Self-centeredness-* The leaders focused on their own egos and were unable to connect with people in the organization to develop their capabilities. There was lack in thinking about doctors, nurses, and all the other people who work directly or indirectly with patients. Whereas, they all need compassion to be able to offer the

care that every patient deserves. Noticing someone's suffering could be difficult, particularly in workplaces where people are busy with their work and preoccupied with their deadlines. Also, depending on the work environment and the culture of the organization, people may tend to hide their pain from others.

2. *Lack of recognition for individual feelings-* There was very little concern for individual experience and people in the organization were condemned, thus preventing from understanding the situation. Rather than creating a win-win situation, there was judgmental attitude in the leadership without looking into the people's feelings. They did not recognize that the experience of a single individual is part of the larger human experience. Judging people in difficulty worsen the situation and condemning them was one of the obstacles for understanding the people and thereby being unable to feel their pain.

3. *Insensitive towards others-*The people felt that the administration was not sensitive to the well-being of others. They failed to notice any change in the behavior of others. The people did not get any support in time of their need due to unconcerned attitude of leaders. Subsequently, it resulted in an environment where people do not feel good about themselves and no effort was from the organization to address the gaps in performance of the people.

4. *No openness to learn –* There were no oneness to learn from the experience of people and leverage their talents for the organization. The leadership was stubborn to think that they know everything. This lead to kill compassion and there was a need of, being open to learn from others for more process-oriented thinking.

5. *Non- empathetic practices-* There was no measure to address the emotional pain of the people and do something to help them who are suffering. No customized actions depending on the personal circumstances to empower and motivate others led to negativity among the people. The defensiveness of the leadership increased further.

Action

ABC leadership looked intentionally on the issues and took appropriate measure to address them. They intended to seek in reducing the level of stress and consequently improve the overall level of staff well-being. They took adequate corrective processes to create a compassionate workplace in which people feel safe to share their problems. They articulated following staff well-being measures to build a compassionate culture in the organization:

1. Valuing the well-being of the people being non-judgmental, with understanding and acknowledging their feelings.
2. Understanding colleagues' pain and problems, and taking action to lessen their suffering.
3. Role-modelling compassion by showing compassion towards colleagues and encouraging team members to do the same.
4. Celebrating, recognizing, and rewarding compassionate actions
5. Encouraging people to share their personal stories of compassion at work to increase empathy and share ideas on how to enhance ABC's compassion capabilities.
6. Promoting healthy practices at work; for example, making time for individual one-to-one meeting.
7. Actively encouraging and empowering others to respond to a colleague's suffering.
8. Making sure that there is a strong connection between people in the respective teams which makes them feel united, sensed, understood, recognized, and supported.
9. Creating a safe environment for the team members to share their personal problems, issues, and challenges.

Some of the activities at an organizational level that foster a compassionate culture included:

- Providing coaching support to leaders so that they model cultural values that support compassion.
- Embedding compassion into organization values.

- Raising awareness about compassion through training and sharing stories of compassionate decisions, or lack of them, and their significance.
- Creating opportunities to bring people together regularly and enable personal connections.

Impact

The leadership of ABC Hospital recognized that creating compassionate workplaces is not an easy task and may require a complete cultural shift. By taking appropriate actions they could encourage gentle changes and adjusting patterns of behavior to avoid similar situations. They realized to create a compassionate organization focusing on individuals and the organization as a whole. They had a willingness to discuss and learn from errors and failures, which resulted in more innovations in this area. They could:

- Reduce defensiveness.
- Achieve successful double-loop learning.
- Improve problem solving.
- Improve staff well-being.
- Improve retention.
- Increase people engagement.
- Encourage innovation.
- Improve people productivity.

Discussion

1. Identifying internal stakeholders of ABC Hospital and their expectation from the leadership?
2. Inscribe the value proposition (promise of value to be delivered, communicated, and acknowledged) of compassionate workplace of ABC Hospital (after corrective measures) that would contribute to its strategic mission (direct achievement of strategic objectives, or contribution toward strategy)?

LEADERSHIP TAKEAWAY

LEADING BY COMPASSION

References:

1. **Worline ,M and Dutton, JE:** *Awakening compassion at work: The quiet power that elevates people and organizations. Berrett-Koehler Publishers, (2017).*

2. **Poorkavoos M** *Towards a more compassionate workplace. DOI: www.roffeypark.com/wp-content/uploads2/Towards-a-more-compassionate-workplace-in-the-events-and-hospitality-sector.pdf , (2017).*

"People are like stained-glass windows. They sparkle and shine when the sun is out, but when the darkness sets in their true beauty is revealed only if there is light from within."- Elisabeth Kübler-Ross

Chapter 7

Strategic Framework of Smart Leadership

Introduction

Smart Leaders leads into the right direction and better understand how to contribute to the bigger picture. Apart from organizing, guiding, and managing; they also join hand with the people and connects a team together through a common purpose. They establish a vision, provide a plan of action, and build strong relationships with their people. They are visionary and lead by encouraging others to reach the desired aspiration together with their best effort. The framework of leadership presents a set of rules, ideas, or beliefs which we use in order to deal with problems or to decide what to do within that context. The leadership framework lay down the underlying structure that helps to understand the selections and changes in our leadership approaches. It provides a way to assess and monitor alterations in leadership approaches that can impact our leadership performance.

Smart Leadership Strategy

The framework of our leadership has to be strategic in nature because it provides a self-improving blueprint that presents the interplay and consistency between, an organization business strategy and various stakeholders. Leadership has a direct cause and effect relationship upon organizations and their success. Leaders determine values, culture, change tolerance, and employee motivation. They shape institutional strategies including their execution and effectiveness. Leadership refers to an individual's ability to influence, motivate, and enable others to contribute toward organizational success. Whereas management involves controlling a group or a set of entities to accomplish a goal. Leaders manage things strategically.

> *"Strategy is about developing and implementing a course of action through inputs based on the assessment of purpose, environment, and creativity to a particular aspiration of output that can be measured in the future, and enable desired outcome."*- **Sanjay Bhattacharya, PhD**

Management may be responsible for implementing tactics and organizing the actions that move a business toward its goals, but it is leadership that sets those goals. Strategic management is a particular course of action that is meant to achieve a corporate goal. It is really significant in defining and setting up the organization's mission, goals, and procedures. Generally, the owners / founders of the organization take the first step in creating a strategic management process. This process is responsible for carrying out several functions such as providing direction and guidance to the employees, setting up measurable goals & a time span to achieve them, and designating duties to all organization personnel.

The strategy for smart leadership entails five key essentials which are discussed as under:

I. **Calling-** Our calling drives us to grow into our own authentic self-hood irrespective of the fact what others think about us to be. People who feel a connection between their personal values and passion generally see their job as a calling. They firm up their commitment to succeed in leveraging their talents for achieving the superior purpose. This is because they want to see the bigger picture of what they are doing. Therefore, calling helps to discover and align our values, passion, talents, and purpose of life; which are the four elements of calling in leadership. It personally means that-
   i. I am able to reflect my values in relation to my role as a vocation.
   ii. I understand that leadership is not a destination, it is a journey and therefore I continue to refine, develop, and build from the foundation.

iii. I am able to develop my talents and exhibit the characteristics most valuable to achieve the set goals.
iv. I am able to align my role with the overall objectives of the organization or group.

Discussion questions:

1. What has been your perspective on "calling" as a leader?
   _____
   _____
   _____

2. How is your perspective on "calling" shaped by your mind-set? By your personality? By the family systems in which you grew up? By the organization you are associated with? How has this perspective impacted your leadership either positively or negatively?
   _____
   _____
   _____

3. On a scale of 1-3 (Would you say you are: 1 -have a real issue, 2 - might need to look at, 3 -doing fairly well); how aware are you of your "calling" on a daily basis? How does this impact your leadership? How can you grow in your awareness about your "calling"?
   _____
   _____
   _____

Objective, Element, Indicator, and Assumption of Calling:

Key Area/ Objective	Element	Indicator	Assumption
Calling/ Articulate the relationship between personal calling and work.	Values	I am able to reflect my values in relation to my role as a vocation.	The consistent demonstration of values form the foundation of credibility.
	Passion	I understand that leadership is not a destination, it is a journey and therefore I continue to refine, develop, and build from the foundation.	We continue to fine-tune our conceptual and experiential understanding of leadership throughout our lifetime.
	Talent	I am able to develop my talents and exhibit the characteristics most valuable to achieve the set goals.	We are capable to learn and develop leadership skills.
	Purpose	I am able to align my role with the overall objectives of the organization or group.	We practice shared responsibility for a common purpose.

Actions:

Few (not limited to) of the actions that display leading by calling may be considered as mentioned below   -

- Prioritize ethics in life.
- Attend to inner urge.
- Step out of comfort zone.
- Learn to do new things by own-self.
- Reflects on experiences to draw out learning.
- Take risks and learn from failure.
- Pursue learning both formally and informally.
- Take note of dreams.
- Maintain identity.
- Continue stability and limit distractions
- Set goals.
- Follow self-morals.

- Identify skills and work on it.
- Seek genuine advice of others.

Outcome:

The expected outcome objective of leading by calling in smart leadership is – "Excelling in personal and professional leadership, as well as supporting the people development."

II. **Competency-** The competence in leadership is the set of evident characteristics and skills that are the enablers for high performance of a job. Competency is a series of knowledge, skills, and attitudes; which contributes effective performance. Leaders play an important role in demonstrating conduct, compliance, considerations, shared responsibilities, and outcomes. They have to ensure not only better job performance but also influence general understanding and satisfaction of all in the organization. They are the role models for others, hence they are supposed to manage themselves by adjusting to the changing environment, think strategically in taking right decisions, and sustain relationship with all stakeholders to achieve organizational goals & objectives. Therefore, we can say that leadership competency is a band of knowledge, skills, and attitude required to influence others with self-management, adaptability, strategic thinking, collaborative relationships, and achieving results; which are the five elements of competency in leadership. It personally means that –

i. I am aware of myself and able to demonstrate ethics and integrity while performing my role.

ii. I clearly understand the organization mission, vision, values, and strategy; to communicate and implement.

iii. I am able to balance tension that occurs between strategic actions and daily tasks that will have a long-term impact on the organization.

iv. I have strong interpersonal skills that promote communication and contributing to the overall morale of a team or group.

v. I am able to evaluate and determine high potential people in the team to deliver results by building their capacity to promote a feeling of fairness among them who may wish to be considered for advancement.

Discussion questions:

1. What has been your perspective on "competency" as a leader?

   _____

2. How is your perspective on "competency" shaped by your mind-set? By your personality? By the family systems in which you grew up? By the organization you are associated with? How has this perspective impacted your leadership either positively or negatively?

   _____

3. On a scale of 1-3 (Would you say you are: 1 -have a real issue, 2 - might need to look at, 3 -doing fairly well); how aware are you of your "competency" on a daily basis? How does this impact your leadership? How can you grow in your awareness about your "competency"?

   _____

Objective, Element, Indicator, and Assumption of Competency:

Key Area / Objective	Element	Indicator	Assumption
Competency / Pursue continuous self-development and achieve greater results through creative action.	Self-management	I am aware of myself and able to demonstrate ethics and integrity while performing my role.	Every one of us is able to handle ourselves and be reliable.
	Adaptability	I clearly understand the organization mission, vision, values, and strategy; to communicate and implement.	We can adapt to new range of behaviours and change our approach of leadership.
	Strategic thinking	I am able to balance tension that occurs between strategic actions and daily tasks that will have a long-term impact on the organization.	Everyone has the capacity to intentionally explore for impact.
	Collaborative relationships	I have strong interpersonal skills that promote communication and contributing to the overall morale of a team or group.	We capitalize on the diverse talents of teams and group members.
	Achieving results	I am able to evaluate and determine high potential people in the team to deliver results by building their capacity to promote a feeling of fairness among them who may wish to be considered for advancement.	We achieve results by building people's capacities.

Actions:

Few (not limited to) of the actions that exhibits leading by competency may be considered as mentioned below:

- Take time to self-reflect.

- Be sensitive towards others.
- Practice taking responsibility.
- Align to the organization culture.
- Clearly articulate core business areas.
- Bring alignment of team goals with organization vision/mission/strategy.
- Build relationships with team.
- Practice making collective decisions.
- Support while delegating tasks.
- Acknowledge others for their contribution.
- Find fulfillment in work through creativity.
- Celebrate success with the team members.

Outcome:

The expected outcome objective of leading by competency in smart leadership is – "Engage people in shared leadership vision for the work, with in depth understanding of business processes."

III. **Commitment-** The commitment is the act of pledging or binding our self to a certain purpose, or to a person, or the organization as the case may be. An effective leader moves followers into action not with coercion but by eliciting their desire and conviction in the vision & goals through articulation. When we commit to the people and things that are truly important to us, our career, or our organization; the results are that - our relationships with people will improve, we will be more successful in achieving our goals, and we will have more time to enjoy our journey. Leadership commitment plays an important role for the achievement of the goals. Commitment urges us gradually explore ourselves because it is a source to transform a capacity into a reality. The belief in our inner self is the foundation of commitment that makes us closer to the accomplishment of goal. Commitment is an intelligent emotional bond of accomplishment. Leaders need to continually evaluate their commitment to - their purpose, people they lead, and organization they work. Therefore, leadership commitment is for the- purpose, people, and organization. The commitment is developed though- continuous persistence, to build influence, and accomplish goals; which are the three elements of commitment in leadership. It personally means that –

i. I am able to be persistent towards my goal or vision that keeps me driving for a higher purpose.
ii. I am able to influence others by my hard work, out of loyalty.
iii. I constantly make new goals or vision and attempt to push my boundaries to achieve more.

Discussion questions:

I. What has been your perspective on "commitment" as a leader?
_____

II. How is your perspective on "commitment" shaped by your mind-set? By your personality? By the family systems in which you grew up? By the organization you are associated with? How has this perspective impacted your leadership either positively or negatively?
_____

III. On a scale of 1-3 (Would you say you are: 1 -have a real issue; 2 - might need to look at; 3 -doing fairly well), how aware are you of your "commitment" on a daily basis? How does this impact your leadership? How can you grow in your awareness about your "commitment"?
_____

Objective, Element, Indicator, and Assumption of Commitment:

Key Area/ Objective	Element	Indicator	Assumption
Commitment/ Ensure strong perseverance for impacting people in realizing results.	Continuous persistence	I am able to be persistent towards my goal or vision that keeps me driving for a higher purpose.	We pursue our dreams assertively.
	Build influence	I am able to influence others by my hard work, out of loyalty.	People are impacted by our dedicated effort.
	Accomplish goals	I constantly make new goals or vision and attempt to push my boundaries to achieve more.	We are motivated by the end result and keep going forward.

Actions:

Few (not limited to) of the actions that reveals leading by commitment may be considered as mentioned below:

- Use inaccuracies as learning opportunities rather than blaming moments.
- Spend time in self-reflection.
- Work alongside with people.
- Let people know they matter by explaining their contribution.
- Encourage people and the team all the time.
- Pick positivity to guide people.
- Set target.
- Catch people doing something right.
- Clarify vision or goals to the people.
- Raise bar/standards for higher accomplishment.

Outcome:

The expected outcome objective of leading by commitment in smart leadership is – "Continuous improvement in leadership approach, though collective action for desired level of accomplishment."

IV. **Confidence-** The confidence is a state of clarity, either in believing that a prediction is correct, or in determining that, a particular course of action is the most effective. It is the feeling or belief in oneself or that one can rely on someone or something. Confident leaders envision positive outcomes no matter what the situation may be. They believe that they have the talent and abilities to lead through an issue for positively impacting the people, team, or organization. They generally tend to have a positive outlook on life, and they have a strong belief in themselves. This belief allows them to take responsible risks and persevere through failures while all the while believing that goals will happen eventually. They constantly shape and guide individuals while making right decisions to keep moving. Therefore, confident leaders process positive thinking which includes- care for people and optimistic approach; have belief in self which includes- trust and sense of control; and take right decisions which includes- original view point and validated information; in leadership role, and these are the three elements of leadership confidence. It personally means that-
   i. Positive action keeps me motivated in achieving my goals by managing challenges better and learning from mistakes.
   ii. I believe in myself about the ability of my team or group for the future course of action and take responsible risks to achieve my personal and professional goals.
   iii. I enter into the right decision-making process with an open mind and do not let my own biases influence them.

Discussion questions:

1. What has been your perspective on "confidence" as a leader?

   _____
   _____
   _____

2. How is your perspective on "confidence" shaped by your mindset? By your personality? By the family systems in which you grew up? By the organization you are associated with? How has this perspective impacted your leadership either positively or negatively?

   _____
   _____
   _____

3. On a scale of 1-3 (Would you say you are: 1 -have a real issue; 2 - might need to look at; 3 -doing fairly well), how aware are you of your "confidence" on a daily basis? How does this impact your leadership? How can you grow in your awareness about your "confidence"?

   _____
   _____
   _____

Objective, Element, Indicator, and Assumption of Confidence:

Key Area/ Objective	Element	Indicator	Assumption
Confidence /Take calculated risk for creativity, innovation, and experimentation; making right choices for superior impact.	Positive thinking	Positive action keeps me motivated in achieving my goals by managing challenges better and learning from mistakes.	Activities focused on positive emotions help us to reach a state of flow.
	Belief in self	I believe in myself about the ability of my team or group for the future course of action and take responsible risks to achieve my personal and professional goals.	We establish courage in the face of challenges.
	Right decision	I enter into the right decision-making process with an open mind and do not let my own biases influence them.	We seek ideas from others to do things differently.

Actions:

Few (not limited to) of the actions that demonstrates leading by confidence may be considered as mentioned below:

- Set realistic goals.
- Reflect on the past achievements.
- Monitor progress.
- Focus on strengths.
- Take constructive feedback from others.
- Learn from mistakes and do not repeat the same.
- Follow through on the task.
- Take responsible risks.
- Do right things and repeat the same.
- Think long term.
- Learn best practices.
- Seek new ideas.
- Question decisions.

Outcome:

The expected outcome objective of leading by confidence in smart leadership is – "Take smart risks with inspiring leadership."

V. **Compassion-** The compassionate person recognizes the concerns of others and then take action to help. When we have compassion we are able to relate to someone's situation, and want to help them by pitching in, for example- we might help someone pick up their groceries if they dropped their shopping basket on the floor. Compassionate leadership is focused on what is best for the individual, the team, and the organization in the long-term. Today, leaders are expected to treat their people with a greater sense of care and humanity to respect the unique attributes and qualities each person bring to the table. It means identifying ourselves with others and being mindful by seeing them as a part of team or organization and relating to what they are experiencing at a much deeper level. Compassionate leader expresses recognition by listening to people. Subsequently they are gratified and cared through support, mentorship, and guidance. People feel inspired to accomplish great things for themselves, their team, or the organization. Compassionate leadership foster people to work together with inclusiveness because of what their leadership mean for the people. Therefore, some of the observed behaviour of compassionate leadership are – go from self to others, create a win-win situation, aspire to understand, learn from others, and exemplify positivity. These behaviours leads to mindfulness, listening ability, inspiring others, and inclusiveness; for achieving the desired results, which are the four elements of compassionate leadership. It personally means that-
   i. I have tremendous willingness to communicate with others more mindfully giving room for them to express themselves.
   ii. I listen to others and make them feel important as an individual.
   iii. I gain trust and confidence of others to inspire them by showing them the willingness to put forth the same effort being asked by others.

iv. I guide people to perform at a high level of excellence by creating a culturally inclusive framework where people work effectively across all functions for collective good.

Discussion questions:

1. What has been your perspective on "compassion" as a leader?

   _____
   _____
   _____

2. How is your perspective on "compassion" shaped by your mindset? By your personality? By the family systems in which you grew up? By the organization you are associated with? How has this perspective impacted your leadership either positively or negatively?

   _____
   _____
   _____

3. On a scale of 1-3 (Would you say you are: 1 -have a real issue; 2 - might need to look at; 3 -doing fairly well), how aware are you of your "compassion" on a daily basis? How does this impact your leadership? How can you grow in your awareness about your "compassion"?

   _____
   _____
   _____

Objective, Element, Indicator, and Assumption of Compassion:

Key Area/ Objective	Element	Indicator	Assumption
Compassion / Understand others and actively listen for all-inclusive approach.	Mindfulness	I have tremendous willingness to communicate with others more mindfully giving room for them to express themselves.	Mindfulness reminds us that each one of us is faced with unique circumstances.
	Listening	I listen to others and make them feel important as an individual.	Listening helps to understand others better.
	Inspiring	I gain trust and confidence of others to enthuse them by showing them the willingness to put forth the same effort being asked by others.	Inspired people feel enthusiastic about their life or their family.
	Inclusiveness	I guide people to perform at a high level of excellence by creating a culturally inclusive framework where people work effectively across all functions for collective good.	Inclusion brings whole people together.

Actions:

Few (not limited to) of the actions that determines leading by compassion may be considered as mentioned below:

- Speak with kindness.
- Apologize for wrong done by self.
- Listen carefully with non-judgemental attitude.
- Say encouraging words to others for better performance.
- Offer to help someone with a task.
- Be happy for someone else's success.
- Accept people as they are and involve all.
- Excuse people for making mistakes.
- Be patient and keep motivating others.
- Show respect and human dignity.
- Express gratitude and appreciation.
- Practice acts of kindness.

- Offer to help someone with their task.

Outcome:

The expected outcome objective of leading by compassion in smart leadership is – "Taking right actions to help others facing hardship."

Framework to Lead Smart

Leaders determine values, culture, change tolerance, and people motivation. They shape organizational strategies including their execution and effectiveness. Smart leaders possess vocation, capability, pledge, self-reliance, and empathy.

"Smart leaders spot their calling, consequently advance their competencies, stay committed, display confidence, and lead compassionately."- **Sanjay Bhattacharya, PhD**

Smart leaders are the role model to lead people, team, or organization. They understand their vocation, sharpen their abilities and are devoted to the task. Further they exhibit coolness focusing on relationship-building with humility. The key essentials of a smart leader are - calling, competency, commitment, confidence, and compassion. They are 5Cs of leading smart.

The 5 Cs of leading smart works in progressive order comprising of- calling; calling contributing to competency; competency contributing to commitment; commitment contributing to confidence; and, confidence contributing to compassion. These key dynamics altogether brands us as smart leaders adding value to empower others, stay authentic, and present ourselves as constant and consistent.

Equations of Smart Leadership

The five Cs of smart leading works together progressively and the missing of any area can lead to failure in consistency to achieve the desired outcomes. It is illustrated in the following equations of smart leadership:

Equations to Lead Smart					
Calling	Competency	Commitment	Confidence	Compassion	= Smart Leader
Calling	Competency	Commitment	Confidence	X	= Lose meaningful connections
Calling	Competency	Commitment	X	Compassion	= Low self-esteem
Calling	Competency	X	Confidence	Compassion	= Waste of time
Calling	X	Commitment	Confidence	Compassion	= Lack of direction
X	Competency	Commitment	Confidence	Compassion	= Disengagement

- A leader may be competent, committed, confident, and compassionate but there will be disengagement within self if there is absence of calling for the role s/he is involved. A disengaged leader is a serious issue and it requires careful assessment and an action plan to re-look on their calling so that they are able to lead from within. Smart leader need to be aligned to what they are supposed to deliver.

- A leader may be having a calling for the job and, also committed towards it with confidence and compassion but may still lack a direction without having competency for that particular role as a smart leader. This may lead to low productivity and seriously have negative impact on the team and the organization. Hence they need to work on their competencies intentionally to produce results; through-orientation towards the desired outcomes, strategic thinking, adaptability, ability to make right decisions, and communicate effectively.

- A leader may be just wasting the time if there is a lack of commitment towards the very cause for which s/he is supposed to lead; even though they may be having a calling, competency, confidence, and compassion within himself or herself. Smart leaders need to be fully involved in the tasks by themselves and developing a link with the people in the teams across the organization to function as a committed leader.

- A leader may be having the calling, competency, commitment, and compassion but still may not be able to perform his or her role effectively without having confidence within himself or herself to be smart. This may lead to a condition where they may lose self - esteem. Therefore, the leaders must be encouraged to learn, by providing plenty of opportunities for additional inputs to sharpen their knowledge and skills. The more knowledge and skills they have to perform their job, the more confident they are going to feel, especially when they approach challenging tasks.

- A leader may lose meaningful connections with the people without compassion within himself or herself; in spite of having the calling, competency, commitment, and confidence. Compassion is very important characteristic of a smart leader because it helps to connect with the people and help them to grow by providing the ideal conditions for doing great work, improving their overall well-being. Hence the leaders must be able to note when people are having a tough time at work or personally, and try to make them feel more comfortable. This also helps to relate to others as well as to ourselves, and making a conscious effort to think and act in a compassionate manner.

Therefore, in order to build leaders to lead smart, it is essential that there should be planned effort to work on all the five Cs which are the keys to lead smart. Smart leaders are the most valuable assets and best things that an organization can get to achieve the highest results through engaged teams.

The strategic framework for five key progressive areas of smart leadership are discussed as under –

1. Leading by Calling:

The strategic framework of calling in smart leadership is cited herewith. Appropriate actions may be taken after self-assessment, to address the gaps of the elements for leading by calling in order to lead smart.

Key Area #	1. Calling	
Objective	Articulate the relationship between personal calling and work.	
Element	Indicator	Assumption
Values	I am able to reflect my values in relation to my role as a vocation	The consistent demonstration of values form the foundation of credibility.
Passion	I understand that leadership is not a destination, it is a journey and therefore I continue to refine, develop, and build from the foundation.	We continue to fine-tune our conceptual and experiential understanding of leadership throughout our lifetime.
Talent	I am able to develop my talents and exhibit the characteristics most valuable to achieve the set goals.	We are capable to learn and develop leadership skills.
Purpose	I am able to align my role with the overall objectives of the organization or group.	We practice shared responsibility for a common purpose.
Expected Outcome	**Excelling in personal and professional leadership, as well as supporting the people development.**	

2. Leading by Competency:

The strategic framework of competency in smart leadership is cited herewith. Appropriate actions may be taken after self-assessment, to address the gaps of the elements for leading by competency in order to lead smart.

Key Area #	2. Competency	
Objective	Pursue continuous self –development and achieve greater results through creative action.	
Element	Indicator	Assumption
Self-management	I am aware of myself and able to demonstrate ethics and integrity while performing my role.	Every one of us is able to handle ourselves and be reliable.
Adaptability	I clearly understand the organization mission, vision, values, and strategy; to communicate and implement.	We can adapt to new range of behaviours and change our approach of leadership.
Strategic thinking	I am able to balance tension that occurs between strategic actions and daily tasks that will have a long-term impact on the organization.	Everyone has the capacity to intentionally explore for impact.
Collaborative relationships	I have strong interpersonal skills that promote communication and contributing to the overall morale of a team or group.	We capitalize on the diverse talents of teams and group members.
Achieving results	I am able to evaluate and determine high potential people in the team to deliver results by building their capacity to promote a feeling of fairness among them who may wish to be considered for advancement.	We achieve results by building people's capacities.
Expected Outcome	Engage people in shared leadership vision for the work, with in depth understanding of business processes.	

3. Leading by Commitment:

The strategic framework of commitment in smart leadership is cited herewith. Appropriate actions may be taken after self-assessment, to address the gaps of the elements for leading by commitment in order to lead smart.

Key Area #	3. Commitment	
Objective	Ensure strong perseverance for impacting people in realizing results.	
Element	Indicator	Assumption
Continuous persistence	I am able to be persistent towards my goal or vision that keeps me driving for a higher purpose.	We pursue our dreams assertively.
Build influence	I am able to influence others by my hard work, out of loyalty.	People are impacted by our dedicated effort.
Accomplish goals	I constantly make new goals or vision and attempt to push my boundaries to achieve more.	We are motivated by the end result and keep going forward.
Expected Outcome	Continuous improvement in leadership approach, though collective action for desired results.	

4. Leading by Confidence:

The strategic framework of confidence in smart leadership is cited herewith. Appropriate actions may be taken after self-assessment, to address the gaps of the elements for leading by confidence in order to lead smart.

Key Area #	4. Confidence	
Objective	Take calculated risk for creativity, innovation, and experimentation; making right choices for superior impact.	
Element	Indicator	Assumption
Positive thinking	*Positive action keeps me motivated in achieving my goals by managing challenges better and learning from mistakes.*	*Activities focused on positive emotions help us to reach a state of flow.*
Belief in self	*I believe in myself about the ability of my team or group for the future course of action and take responsible risks to achieve my personal and professional goals.*	*We establish courage in the face of challenges.*
Right decision	*I enter into the right decision-making process with an open mind and do not let my own biases influence them.*	*We seek ideas from others to do things differently.*
Expected Outcome	**Take smart risks with inspiring leadership.**	

5. Leading by Compassion:

The strategic framework of compassion in smart leadership is cited herewith. Appropriate actions may be taken after self-assessment, to address the gaps of the elements for leading by compassion in order to lead smart.

Key Area #	5. Leading By Compassion	
Objective	Understand others and actively listen for all-inclusive approach.	
Element	Indicator	Assumption
Mindfulness	I have tremendous willingness to communicate with others more mindfully giving room for them to express themselves.	Mindfulness reminds us that each one of us is faced with unique circumstances.
Listening	I listen to others and make them feel important as an individual.	Listening helps to understand others better.
Inspiring	I gain trust and confidence of others to enthuse them by showing them the willingness to put forth the same effort being asked by others.	Inspired people feel enthusiastic about their life or their family.
Inclusiveness	I guide people to perform at a high level of excellence by creating a culturally inclusive framework where people work effectively across all functions for collective good.	Inclusion brings whole people together.
Expected Outcome	Taking right actions to help others facing hardship.	

Conclusion

Leadership is a practice where the leader develops a vision and the strategy through inputs based on the assessment of purpose, environment, and creativity to a particular aspiration of output that can be measured in the future, and enable desired outcome. Smart leaders remain competitive in a changing environment.

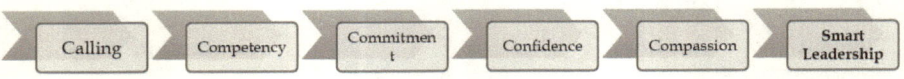

Smart leadership is sequentially organized around five key areas of leadership - calling, competency, commitment, confidence, and compassion. These keys must always be considerations when exercising leadership to enhance the prospects of long –term realization. At different moments they affect each other differently, as they are the five keys of leadership success that drives us to lead smart.

LEADERSHIP TAKEAWAY

STRTEGIC FRAMEWORK OF SMART LEADERSHIP

References:

1. Wooll, Maggie :Trying to find your calling, Better up ,June 2022.
2. Indeed Editorial Team: How To Develop Core Leadership Competencies (With Tips), Feb 2023.
3. https://leadershipfreak.blog/2012/09/12/20-commitments-that-enhance-leadership.
4. Bridges, Frances: Ways To Build Confidence, Forbes; July 2017.
5. Cherry, Kendra: https://www.verywellmind.com/what-is-compassion-5207366, Nov 2021.

Index

Chapter 1

Smart Leading

- Key Essentials of Smart Leading   2
  - Calling   3
  - Competency   4
  - Commitment   6
  - Confidence   7
  - Compassion   *8*

Chapter 2

Leading by Calling

- Elements of Calling in Leadership   26
  - Values   27
  - Passion   27
  - Talent   28
  - Purpose   *28*

Chapter 3

Leading by Competency

  - *Components of Competency*   39
- Elements of Competency in Leadership   41
  - Self-management   42
  - Adaptability   43
  - Strategic thinking   43
  - Collaborative relationships   44
  - Achieving results   45

Chapter 4

Leading by Commitment

- Forms of Leadership Commitment 56
  - Commitment to the purpose 57
  - Commitment to the people 57
  - Commitment to the organization 58

- Elements of Commitment in Leadership 58
  - Continuous persistence 59
  - Build influence 60
  - Accomplish goals 61

Chapter 5

Leading by Confidence 65

- Elements of Confidence in Leadership 71
  - Positive thinking 71
    - ✓ *Care for people* 72
    - ✓ *Optimistic approach* 72
  - Belief in self 72
    - ✓ *Trust* 73
    - ✓ *Sense of control* 73
  - Right decision 73
    - ✓ *Original viewpoint* 73
    - ✓ *Validated information* 74

Chapter 6

Leading by Compassion 82

- Behaviors of Compassionate Leaders 83
  - Go from self to others 84
  - Create a win-win situation 85

-	Aspire to understand	85
-	Learn from others	86
-	Exemplify positivity	86

- Elements of Compassion in Leadership — 88

  - Mindfulness — 88
  - Listening — 89
  - Inspiring — 90
  - Inclusiveness — 90

Chapter 7

Strategic Framework of Smart Leadership — 100

- Smart Leadership Strategy — 100

  - Calling — 101
  - Competency — 104
  - Commitment — 107
  - Confidence — 110
  - Competence — 113

- Framework to Lead Smart — 116
  - *Equations of Smart Leadership* — *117*

www.ingramcontent.com/pod-product-compliance
Lightning Source LLC
LaVergne TN
LVHW041609070526
838199LV00052B/3052